Delia's

FRUGAL FOOD

Delia's
FRUGAL FOOD

First published in Great Britain in 1976 by Hodder & Stoughton
New editions 1987 and 1997
This edition published in 2008 by Hodder & Stoughton
An Hachette Livre UK company

2

A CIP catalogue record for this title is available from the British Library

Hardback ISBN 978 0 340 91856 2
Trade Paperback ISBN 978 0 340 91857 9

Project editor Lesley Levene
Photographs by Jeff Cottenden
Line illustrations by Elizabeth Hallett
Text design by Craig Burgess
Typeset by Hewer Text UK Ltd, Edinburgh
Printed and bound by Graphicom, Italy

Typeset in Sabon, Futura and Mrs Eaves

Hodder & Stoughton policy is to use papers that are natural, renewable
and recyclable products and made from wood grown in sustainable forests.
The logging and manufacturing processes are expected to conform to the
environmental regulations of the country of origin.

Hodder & Stoughton Ltd
338 Euston Road
London NW1 3BH

www.hodder.co.uk

contents

frugal again

WHAT GOES AROUND COMES AROUND. Re-reading this book thirty-two years after it was originally published, I find it has an eerily familiar ring to it. After periods of such affluence that we were being urged not to throw so much away, we are now once again facing cutbacks and shortages.

This time round, though, the reasons are much more complex and serious. Climate change is forcing us to stand back and review how much food we've become used to throwing away. An astonishing one-third of the food we buy is wasted, and the cost in energy emissions in merely producing unwanted waste is equivalent to taking one car in five off UK roads.

Personally I feel there can be a positive response to all this – perhaps because I remember rationing and how just having a couple of ounces of sweets a week was a far more pleasurable experience than having wall-to-wall confectionery everywhere you look. I would even say frugal can be fun when it takes us back to the roots of our cooking – the luxury, say, of home-made soup as opposed to the blandness of a chilled variety (not to mention the astonishing difference in price).

Apart from the lovely new artwork, *Frugal Food* is being presented just as it was, with a minimum of tweaking, as we felt it had a certain nostalgic appeal in showing how things were thirty-two years ago. The book has remained a favourite for many over the years, and it is now my hope that a new generation faced with rising food costs will also find it helpful.

Delia Smith
2008

Author's royalties from the sale of this book will go to the Catholic Fund for Overseas Development (www.cafod.org.uk).

WE HAVE CERTAINLY JUMPED through a few nutritional hoops since 1976. Don't eat animal fat. Only eat vegetable fat. Don't eat vegetable fat that's hydrogenated. So back to butter, everyone, it's not the killer we once thought it was. Olive oil has escaped the wrath of nutritionists so far, transformed from a medicinal item available only at the chemist's to a bewildering array of varieties from around the world.

In the original edition of *Frugal Food* there were many more references to BEEF, PORK or LAMB DRIPPING, BACON FAT and LARD. This was because real cooks, who collected these in bowls, knew how their flavour could enhance so many dishes, as well as save money on cooking fats and oil. To replace these, I suggest using groundnut oil as a good all-rounder which is less expensive than olive oil.

There has been an about-turn with EGGS too in the meantime. We started with small, medium and large, then we moved on to 1, 2 or 3. Now we're back to size, but all the eggs in these recipes are large.

We can now buy a wide range of MILK, not just whole milk as in the old days, so the recipes have been changed to specify semi-skimmed. As for TOP OF THE MILK, what a memory! Instead, where a little cream is called for, half-fat crème fraîche, with its easy storage and longer shelf life, is what to use.

At the time of writing *Frugal Food*, people mostly made their own PASTRY and needed to know the proportion of flour to fat. Today ready-made pastry is widely available, so I have indicated the total weight as well (for example, 175g flour and 75g fat is the equivalent of 250–275g ready-made).

CURRY POWDER has been very variable over the years, but the best at present is Seasoned Pioneers Madras curry powder, which comes in resealable bags that exclude air and light, preserving them longer, and so saves money. They also stock all the individual spices used in this book (see www.seasonedpioneers.co.uk).

DRIED HERBS crop up in *Frugal Food* because that's all you could get then. A good modern all-round alternative – still cheaper than buying fresh – would be dried Herbes de Provence (also from Seasoned Pioneers).

introduction

ANYONE WHO WANTS TO, or is forced to, live *really* frugally (that is to say, at subsistence level) has no need of a cookbook. And at the same time I'm quite sure there are many people who, because they are careful, can live more frugally than this book would suggest.

Who, then, is this book for? Quite simply for people like myself, those who have lived and cooked during the affluent years and now find themselves caught up in the spiral of inflation, rising prices and impending world food shortages.

In short, it's a *start*. If you wish to trim your cooking (and spending) wings a bit, start here. It's quite easy, quite fun and, if my experience in preparing and writing this book is anything to go by, it's really not half so morbid an exercise as you might think. In fact, once you become really calculating, boring old shopping can take on a new meaning.

No more will you simply go through the motions of loading up the supermarket trolley and day-dreaming in dreary checkout queues. You'll go forth into battle fortified, as it were, by the armour of your new-found attention to frugality! The seductive cunning of commercials will now meet its match – in you. Nothing will be tossed lightly into your basket: you'll know how much it weighs, what it costs *and* how much it cost last week.

You haven't got the time? I know, I said it too. But actually I'm not so sure that all this time-saving really works. I once watched a lady standing in a long checkout queue with just a large bag of prepared Brussels sprouts (they were at the time about 30 per cent dearer than the fresh ones). She was in the queue for a good ten or twelve minutes; she could, had she so wished, have sat in her own kitchen and peeled fresh Brussels sprouts in the same time. Then take something like tea bags: they'll save you the bother of emptying tea leaves – whatever small amount of time that involves – but you'll pay twice the price for your tea.

However, before we start cooking, here are a few tips on thinking frugally.

the cheap
charter

1. YOUR MONEY OR YOUR TIME. Really this is what is at the root of many of our economic predicaments. 'Labour-saving' was the slogan of the 60s: leave it all to the kitchen gadgets, the machines, the tins and packets, and put your feet up. Well, even if you overlook the psychological repercussions for bored (if liberated) housewives, consider the economic implications for a minute. First of all, instant foods cost a fortune. Secondly, all those super gadgets cost a fortune – and then they break down, and when they do it's ten to one you can't get the repair man to come. 'Are you north or south Suffolk, madam?' 'Oh, you're in the middle. He won't be in your area for ten days.' So off you go to the launderette, get a parking ticket, plus the call-out charge for the man when he comes ten days later and the cost of the spare part. Just one (real-life) example of how much saved labour we have to pay for. The same applies to cooking: if you are willing to spend the *time,* you are bound to save money.

2. GETTING OUT OF THE SUPERMARKET AND BACK INTO THE KITCHEN. So our bored, liberated housewife needs a job (*a*) to pay for her labour-saving home and (*b*) to pay the interest. With the result that on Friday nights and Saturdays the supermarkets are packed with rushed, harassed working wives and mothers stocking up on instant puds, apple pies, sponge cakes, frozen hamburgers, fish fingers and packaged meat, to name but a few expensive items. A few years ago I wrote a book to enable people to make the very best of all these things. But in the meantime our priorities, I feel, have been changing, and it is the kitchen now that demands more of our time and imagination. Hence the aim of this book – to make that time spent as interesting and worthwhile as possible.

3. SEASONAL SENSE. I need hardly mention how the price of oil has affected everything we consume, but just *think* how much more it now costs to fly all those tasteless out-of-season fruits and vegetables merely so we can buy whatever we want every single week of the year! Not only has

this jet-set food eclipsed the natural cycles of our diet, but also it has become so much harder to decide what to cook when there's absolutely everything to choose from. Nature is perfectly capable of providing us with a varied and interesting diet throughout the year, and by buying things in their natural season you'll be getting them at their most plentiful and therefore at their cheapest. In June a few ungraded asparagus spears can be far cheaper than imported celery; in December home-grown celery is much less expensive (and has far more flavour) than a pound of imported tomatoes. And, personally, I enjoy the fun of anticipation – I long for the first tender young peas, and equally I look forward to the (so underrated) root vegetables of winter.

4. ANTI FREEZE. Well, I'm afraid I am, although I admit it's a personal thing largely for the reasons outlined above. Also I'm not convinced freezing does always save money. Each time I am reminded that 20 per cent of the population are freezer-owners I console myself with the thought that there are still 80 per cent who are not. My main grumble is that unless you understand temperature control with almost scientific dedication freezing causes *loss of flavour*, and as a cook I spend a great deal of time and effort nurturing flavour. One report in a consumer magazine pointed out that very often freezer families spent more on meat than other families – they bought more than they normally would in order to justify the freezer, and of course when buying whole sides they were landed with far more heads, tails and ears than they needed. Having said all this, it is true you *can* save a little money with fruit and vegetables, if you grow these yourself and produce too much for your immediate needs. If you already have a freezer and it's saving you money, it can't be a bad thing. But if you don't and are thinking about it, ask yourself if you really want to eat your courgettes and strawberries in January and your red cabbage in June.

I think it is only fair to point out that since this was written the advent of blast-freezing has transformed the quality – and range – of frozen products.

5. SAVING IT. Energy has become a fashionable word of late. Before that saving kitchen energy meant sitting down to shell the peas. When the government first urged us daily to switch something off, we listened a bit;

then the enormous increases in charges started arriving through our letter boxes and we listened a lot. After water and heating, the oven is the highest consumer of energy in the house, and heating up the whole capacity of the oven just to cook a quiche is no longer feasible. No doubt you all have devised ways of saving energy in the kitchen, but here anyway are a few suggestions:

(a) *Keep the kettle regularly descaled – it will boil quicker.*

(b) *Invest in a steamer and cook one vegetable on top of another on the same heat.*

(c) *When baking jacket potatoes, push a skewer through the centres as this conducts the heat to the insides and speeds up the cooking time.*

(d) *Invest in an electric toaster – it uses far less energy than the grill.*

(e) *Try to use the oven to its capacity by planning to use it for more than one thing (e.g. baking in a batch, cooking two casseroles or cooking vegetables and soups in the oven if it's on).*

(f) *If you are buying a new oven, consider a double one so that you can use the smaller oven for most things and probably cut costs by half.*

6. A TOUCH OF SPICE. One way to prevent life getting dull when you're saving money on cooking is to stock up with a few herbs and spices. Don't get me wrong: throwing in a hotch-potch of this and that is definitely not recommended. It is the subtle addition that gives a touch of luxury to the simplest dishes. First and foremost (I'll say it yet again), do invest in a pepper mill. Freshly ground black pepper adds a new dimension instantly to your cooking. Also keep some untreated pure rock salt (such as Maldon) in your spice cupboard – it's more expensive than table salt but, because it's saltier, it goes further. Coarsely ground black pepper and a sprinkling of crushed rock salt can put something like egg and chips in the four-star class! Spices are cheaper sold loose or in packets. Why pay for fancy jars? At the same time pester your local delicatessen or wholefood shop for unusual spices – the more we ask, the more we're likely to get them.

Green-fingered cooks, or even those who aren't (like me), should be able to grow fresh herbs, either in the garden or on a sunny windowsill in pots. There are a number of very informative books available.

Finally, one thing that I used to get a lot of letters about was olive oil and its price. It *is* delicious, but I agree that it is very expensive. A good alternative is groundnut oil, which I like because it has little flavour of its own and therefore doesn't mask other flavours, like some abominable oils on the market at present. Groundnut oil is good for frying – and add a knob of butter for flavour.

I also use groundnut oil in salad dressing and in mayonnaise with a little crushed garlic added, again for flavour. If you have some precious olive oil, you can make it go further by adding 50 per cent groundnut oil to it. For my vinaigrette dressing I use 1 tablespoon of wine or cider vinegar, 6–7 tablespoons of oil, 1 crushed clove of garlic, 1 teaspoon of mustard, 1 teaspoon of crushed rock salt and freshly milled black pepper – then I shake everything together vigorously in a screw-top jar. In the summer a few chopped herbs will give it an extra-special flavour.

7. **HOW TO COOK WITHOUT WINE.** I think it was Elizabeth David, one of our greatest cookery writers, who once said that if the British spent as much money on wine in the kitchen as they do on gravy powder, meat cubes and instant stock they would all enjoy better food. Well, I heartily endorse that, but just as all those chemically flavoured aids have gone up in price, so too has wine. But, again prompted by Mrs David, I have discovered that a very good alternative to wine in the kitchen is dry cider. In fact, I now rarely use wine, but I always have some dry cider handy for special dishes. I've experimented quite a lot and have found that a classic coq au vin or even boeuf bourguignon (see the version on page 84) has turned out beautifully with dry cider.

8. **A QUESTION OF CREAM.** As a cookery writer I can say quite confidently that nothing seems to get people's economical backs up quite as much as cream in cooking. It's perfectly all right to spend money on smoking, or crisps, or bars of chocolate, but cooking with cream is considered by some to be the ultimate in kitchen extravagance. One lady was outraged, I recall, by my making a bread and butter pudding on television with cream; I ought to have been teaching people to economise in this day and age. Well, perhaps in the context of this book the appearance of a little cream here and there does call for an explanation. For me, quite simply, cream is the one ingredient that makes frugality tolerable! If you like, you can substitute top of the milk for it.

9. **WHAT ARE WE LEAVING?** In one American university there is, would you believe, a department of Garbageology which regularly 'borrows' people's dustbins and analyses their contents. They claim that it tells us a great deal about our modern way of life. In one American city they discovered that the average family wasted 10–15 per cent of all the food it bought (amounting in the whole city, over the year, to $10 million worth of food thrown away). And that was not bones, scraps or peelings but large pieces of once perfectly edible bread and meat, as well as unopened packs of vegetables and television dinners. They even found that, as the price of meat soared, so did the wastage! I mention all this only to underline the obvious point that frugality calls for good management, and an enthusiastic approach to leftovers (for which you'll find some recipes later). It would be a tragic waste of that extra time we're going to spend in the kitchen if 15 per cent of the food was thrown away afterwards.

conversion tables

All these are approximate conversions, which have been rounded up or down. All spoon measurements used throughout this book are level unless specified otherwise.

oven temperatures

140°C	275°F	1
150	300	2
170	325	3
180	350	4
190	375	5
200	400	6
220	425	7
230	450	8
240	475	9

measurements

3mm	$1/8$ inch
5mm	$1/4$
1cm	$1/2$
2	$3/4$
2.5	1
3	$1^1/4$
4	$1^1/2$
4.5	$1^3/4$
5	2
6	$2^1/2$
7.5	3
9	$3^1/2$
10	4
13	5
13.5	$5^1/4$
15	6
16	$6^1/2$
18	7
19	$7^1/2$
20	8
23	9
24	$9^1/2$
25.5	10
28	11
30	12

weights

10g	$1/2$oz
20	$3/4$
25	1
40	$1^1/2$
50	2
60	$2^1/2$
75	3
110	4
125	$4^1/2$
150	5
175	6
200	7
225	8
250	9
275	10
350	12
450	1lb
700	$1^1/2$
900	2
1.35kg	3

volume

55ml	2fl oz
75	3
150	5 ($1/4$ pint)
275	$1/2$ pint
570	1
725	$1^1/4$
1 litre	$1^3/4$
1.2	2
1.5	$2^1/2$
2.25	4

luxury
soups

So how can we be at once frugal and luxurious, you're thinking? Easy.

Luxuries are rarities – foie gras and caviar cost a fortune because they're scarce. When oysters were ten-a-penny (as indeed they were in generations past) they were merely food of the poor; now they're right up in the luxury class.

One of the rarest things in these days of instant living, in my opinion, is real home-made soup made with real home-made stock – and for me that makes it a luxury. At least this state of affairs has a positive side for us frugal cooks, because now we can offer our family or friends luxury at a very small cost.

I'll go even further. If you've got an attractive tureen full of comforting, inviting home-made soup on the table – with home-made bread, butter, a hunk of cheese and some fruit – who's going to notice the absence of meat or fish or any other main course? In this chapter I've chosen, for the most part, substantial and filling soups, and just a couple of lighter ones with the summer months in mind.

basic stock

1.8kg beef shin bones (in pieces)
450g veal knuckle bones (in pieces)
1 Spanish onion, peeled and quartered
2 large carrots, scraped and cut into large chunks
2 sticks celery (plus leaves), cut into halves
1 bay leaf
1 blade of mace
10 whole black peppercorns
1 small bunch parsley stalks
1 heaped teaspoon salt
1 teaspoon sugar

Preheat the oven to 230°C/450°F/gas mark 8.

First of all place the bones in a meat roasting tin together with the onion and carrots, and place the tin on the highest shelf in the oven. Leave it for about 45 minutes to allow the bones and vegetables to brown, turning them now and then so that they colour evenly. Then have some boiling water ready, and transfer the bones, the onion and carrots to a cooking pot (about 6.8 litres capacity).

Add 4 litres of water to the pot, along with the celery, bay leaf, mace, peppercorns and parsley stalks, and bring the liquid very slowly up to simmering point before adding the salt and sugar. Skim off any scum that has come to the surface, partly cover and simmer as gently as possible for 4–5 hours (partly covering the pot by putting the lid half on will ensure the liquid reduces to give the stock a more concentrated flavour).

When it's ready, strain into a clean pan and leave to cool. When the stock is quite cold you can then remove the layer of fat that will have formed on the top. The stock is now ready for use; the bones can be either discarded or topped up with more water. This is a basic brown beef stock. For a light stock, use all veal bones instead of beef and dispense with the browning in the oven.

goulash soup with dumplings

450g shin of beef
2 tablespoons beef dripping
1 large onion, peeled and chopped
2 tablespoons plain flour
1 tablespoon Hungarian paprika
1/4 teaspoon Herbes de Provence
1/2 teaspoon caraway seeds
1 clove garlic, crushed
1 x 400g tin Italian tomatoes
850ml beef stock
1 teaspoon tomato purée
450g potatoes, peeled and cut into cubes
1 green pepper, deseeded and chopped
150ml soured cream or natural yoghurt

For the dumplings:
110g self-raising flour
50g shredded suet
Seasoning

Trim and cut the meat into very small pieces, then heat the beef dripping in a large pan and fry the meat over a high heat until well browned. Now lower the heat a little, stir in the onion and cook until it's lightly browned. Sprinkle in the flour, paprika, Herbes de Provence, caraway seeds and garlic. Stir well and cook for a minute or two before adding the tomatoes and stock. When it comes to simmering point, cover and continue simmering very gently for 45 minutes. After that, take the lid off and stir in the tomato purée, followed by the potatoes and chopped pepper, and simmer gently for 10 minutes, stirring occasionally. Meanwhile, in a bowl, mix the flour and shredded suet, season and add enough cold water to make a smooth, elastic dough. Divide the dough into 12 small dumplings, pop them into the soup – don't press them down, though, just let them float. Then put the lid back on and simmer for a further 25 minutes. Taste to check the seasoning and add a dollop of soured cream or yoghurt to each serving.

split pea and vegetable soup

Yellow or green split peas will do for this deliciously thick and substantial soup.

225g green split peas, washed
75g butter
110g streaky bacon, rinded and chopped small
1 medium onion, peeled and chopped
2 sticks celery, chopped
1 large carrot, scraped and chopped
1/2 small turnip, peeled and chopped
1/2 small swede, peeled and chopped
1.7 litres stock (or water)
Seasoning

First, in a large cooking pot, melt the butter, then cook the bacon and onion in it for 5 minutes before adding the rest of the vegetables. Give them a good stir round and let them colour a little at the edges over a fairly low heat. Then pour in the stock and add the washed split peas. Bring everything back to simmering point, skim the surface if there's any scum, put a lid on and continue to simmer very gently for about 1½ hours, or until the peas are absolutely soft. Now liquidise the soup just a little (or else sieve it) – it shouldn't be too uniformly smooth. Taste, season, reheat and serve the soup garnished with some croutons crisp-fried in butter.

NOTE: *There's no need to soak the split peas, but the length of cooking time may vary 30 minutes or so either way.*

thick country soup

I say thick, because you could stand your spoon up in this one! If you prefer it a
little thinner, just add more liquid, to your taste.

225g dried haricot beans
2 tablespoons oil
1 onion, peeled and chopped
2 cloves garlic, crushed
2 sticks celery, chopped
2 carrots, scraped and chopped
110g streaky bacon, rinded and chopped
2 leeks, cleaned thoroughly, trimmed, halved lengthways and sliced into 5mm rings
3 courgettes, unpeeled but trimmed each end and chopped
½ small head savoy cabbage, shredded
2 teaspoons Herbes de Provence
4 tablespoons tomato purée
110ml long-grain rice
Seasoning

First, put the beans into a saucepan with 1.7 litres of cold water, bring to the boil
and boil for 2–3 minutes. Then turn the heat off, put a lid on and leave on one
side for about an hour, to soak. Towards the end of that time, heat the oil in a
large pan and gently fry the onion, garlic, celery, carrots and bacon together for
about 10–15 minutes. Now return to the soaked beans: bring them back to the
boil with the lid on and simmer for about 30 minutes, or until they are tender.
Then, using a draining spoon, scoop out about half the beans and transfer them
to an electric blender. Measure and add 570ml of their cooking water, blending
until smooth; then pour this on to the softened vegetables. Add the remaining
whole beans and their cooking water, together with the prepared leeks, courgettes,
cabbage, Herbes de Provence and a further 570ml of water. Bring it all to the boil,
add the tomato purée and sprinkle in the rice. Stir well, then cover and simmer
very gently for 30 minutes. Finally, taste and season well.

german soup
with frankfurters

This soup is made more substantial by the addition of bacon and frankfurters.

1.2 litres stock – preferably home-made
2 medium potatoes, peeled and diced
4 leeks
225g turnips
225g carrots
1 stick celery
110g streaky bacon, rinded and chopped
4 long frankfurters (or 6 small)
Seasoning

Pour the stock into a largish saucepan with the diced potatoes and bring to the boil; then cover and simmer gently until the potatoes are soft – that should be in about 10 minutes. While this is happening, start to prepare the vegetables: first the leeks, which should be slit open lengthways and then cut across in 5mm slices. Wash them in several changes of water to get rid of the dirt, then drain in a colander. Now take a sharp knife and peel and dice the root vegetables into quite small pieces, and cut up the celery too. The chopped bacon should be fried without any additional fat until it's fairly crisp. Then, as soon as the potatoes are soft, rub them through a sieve (or liquidise them) and return them to the saucepan together with the vegetables, bacon and any fat that came out of it. Now bring the soup up to a gentle simmer, taste and add some seasoning, then cover and cook gently for about an hour. The frankfurters should be sliced thinly and stirred into the soup to heat through gently just a few minutes before you are ready to eat. Serve it very hot.

soupe les halles

Serves 6

2 tablespoons butter, plus a little extra
2 tablespoons oil
700g onions, peeled and thinly sliced
2 cloves garlic, crushed
1/2 teaspoon granulated sugar
1.5 litres good beef stock
6 slices French bread (baked till crisp for about 20 minutes in a medium oven)
225g Cheddar or Lancashire cheese, grated
Seasoning

Heat the butter and oil together in a large saucepan. Stir in the sliced onions, garlic and sugar, and cook over a fairly low heat for about 30 minutes, or until the base of the pan is covered with a nutty brown, caramelised film (this browning process is important as it improves the colour of the resulting soup and also helps considerably with the flavour). Now pour on the stock, bring to the boil, cover and simmer gently for about an hour. Then taste the soup and season.

Preheat the grill. Now spread the slices of baked French bread with butter. Place each slice in a fireproof soup bowl and ladle in the soup, then when the bread surfaces sprinkle grated cheese over the top of each bowl. Place the bowls under a hot grill until the cheese is browned and bubbling.

potage flamande

This is nicest made with young Brussels sprouts in November – hopefully after a good frost.

350g potatoes
2 leeks
350g Brussels sprouts
50g butter
420ml stock
570ml semi-skimmed milk
2 tablespoons half-fat crème fraîche
Seasoning
A squeeze of lemon juice
4 rashers streaky bacon, rinded

Peel and slice the potatoes first; then halve the leeks lengthways, slice them across fairly thickly and wash and drain them thoroughly. Then trim the bases of the sprouts and discard any damaged outer leaves. Now quarter the larger sprouts and halve the smaller ones. Next melt the butter in a good large saucepan. Add the potatoes, leeks and sprouts, and stir well to coat them nicely in the butter. Cover and cook gently for 5 minutes, then add the stock and milk. Bring to simmering point, cover and cook *very* gently for 20–25 minutes, or until the potatoes are soft. Now liquidise or sieve the soup and return it to the pan. Add the crème fraîche, then reheat the soup gently, taste and season, adding a squeeze of lemon juice. The bacon should be grilled until absolutely crisp, then crumbled into the soup before serving.

potage paysanne

I often make this with the stock left over from boiling a bacon joint.

¼ medium turnip, peeled
½ small swede, peeled
2 carrots, scraped
2 sticks celery
2 medium onions, peeled
1 large or 2 small leeks, trimmed and washed
A good handful of green Brussels tops (or the inner leaves of a green cabbage)
1 dessertspoon butter
1 clove garlic, crushed
570ml–1.2 litres stock (or half stock, half water)
2 teaspoons tomato purée
Seasoning

First take a chopping board and a sharp knife and chop all the vegetables very finely – the soup is not going to be sieved, so it's important that the vegetables are cut very small. Now take a large cooking pot, melt the butter and stir in all the chopped vegetables except the Brussels tops. Stir them round and round to get a good coating of butter, then add the garlic, put a lid on and let them sweat over a low heat for about 15 minutes – don't worry if they turn a little golden round the edges, but *do* stir them now and then to prevent them from sticking. After that, pour in the stock and add the tomato purée. Cover again and simmer gently for 45 minutes, before adding the shredded greens. Taste and season, then cook for a further 10 minutes, this time without a lid.

cream of celery soup

I think this is a delicious soup – best made with English celery after a good
November frost.

350g sticks celery, trimmed (save the leaves)
25g butter
110g potatoes, peeled and cut into chunks
2 medium leeks (white parts only), sliced and washed
570ml chicken stock
275ml semi-skimmed milk
1/4 teaspoon celery seeds
2 tablespoons cream
Seasoning

Melt the butter in a large pan over a low heat. Chop the celery and add it to the
pan, together with the potatoes and drained leeks. Then stir to coat the vegetables
with butter, cover and cook very gently for about 15 minutes, shaking the pan
from time to time to prevent the vegetables from sticking. Next pour in the stock
and milk, and sprinkle in the celery seeds and some salt. Bring to simmering
point, then cover and cook over a very low heat (watching it doesn't boil over) for
20–25 minutes, or until the vegetables are absolutely tender. Then liquidise or
sieve the soup, return the purée to the pan and add the cream. Bring back to the
boil, taste and season, then just before serving chop up the reserved celery leaves
and stir them into the soup.

carrot and leek soup

This makes a nice change from the more usual Leek and Potato Soup, provided of course the carrots are not too expensive.

450g leeks
450g carrots
1 medium onion
1 dessertspoon butter
1 clove garlic, crushed
1.5 litres stock
Seasoning
A dash of Worcestershire sauce

First of all prepare the vegetables. The leeks should be trimmed, leaving as much green as possible, then halved lengthways, chopped and washed in plenty of cold water. Then scoop them into a colander to drain. Next peel the carrots and cut them into smallish pieces – and the same goes for the onion. Now take a large saucepan, heat the butter and add all the prepared vegetables along with the crushed clove of garlic. Stir them around a bit, then cover and sweat them for 10 minutes over a low heat, shaking the pan from time to time. Next pour in the stock, add some seasoning, bring to simmering point, cover and simmer very gently for about 10 minutes, or until the pieces of carrot are tender. Now either sieve or liquidise the soup, then return it to the pan, taste to check the seasoning, add a few drops of Worcestershire sauce and reheat gently. If you happen to have some Parmesan cheese handy, a little would be very nice sprinkled on each serving.

potato soup
with bacon

This is a thick, very warming soup, just right when the weather is cold.

450g potatoes, peeled and chopped
2 large carrots, scraped and chopped
2 sticks celery, chopped
1 small turnip, peeled and chopped
1 medium onion, peeled and chopped
1 dessertspoon butter
1.2 litres stock
$^{1}/_{2}$ teaspoon Herbes de Provence
Seasoning
2 rashers streaky bacon, rinded

Take a large thick-based saucepan and melt the butter over a very gentle heat.
Then add all the prepared vegetables, stirring them around to get them well
coated. Cover with a tight-fitting lid, and with the heat kept very low let the
vegetables sweat gently for about 15 minutes – if you give the pan a shake from
time to time you won't have any trouble with them sticking. After 15 minutes pour
in the stock and add the Herbes de Provence and some seasoning. Then put the lid
almost back on but leave a 1cm gap at the edge (to let some of the steam escape).
Simmer the soup like this for about another 20 minutes, or until the vegetables are
soft. Now you can either sieve or liquidise half the contents of the saucepan, and
then return them to the other half. This means that the soup will be thickened
nicely and will still have some bits of vegetable in it for texture. Next, grill or fry
the bacon rashers until crisp, and crumble them into the soup in little bits. I think
this soup is nice served with some croutons crisp-fried in butter.

cauliflower soup

As cauliflowers are available all the year round and prices tend to fluctuate enormously, this soup is only really economical when the price is right.

1 largish cauliflower
570ml stock (a light chicken stock or just plain water)
1 bay leaf
570ml semi-skimmed milk
350g potatoes, peeled and chopped small
A squeeze of lemon juice
Seasoning
Freshly grated nutmeg
1 tablespoon cream, half-fat crème fraîche or soured cream (whatever's available)

First separate the florets of the cauliflower from the hard stalk (this can be kept and grated for a salad). Now you need to separate the florets themselves into very tiny pieces. Then in a medium saucepan bring the stock and bay leaf to simmering point, throw in the little pieces of cauliflower and simmer them for about 6 minutes, or until they are just cooked but still have some 'bite'. Lift them out with a draining spoon and keep them on one side. Pour in the milk now and add the potatoes, then simmer gently without a lid until the potatoes are soft – about 10 minutes. Next rub the soup through a sieve, or liquidise it, and return it to the saucepan. Now return the cauliflower to the saucepan and reheat gently, adding a squeeze of lemon juice, some seasoning, and a scraping of nutmeg. Then stir in the cream just before serving.

soupe au chou

The reason this has a French title is, as well as being French-inspired, Soupe au Chou sounds more promising than Bacon and Cabbage Soup.

½ white cabbage
1 dessertspoon butter
225g unsmoked streaky bacon, rinded and diced
2 medium onions, peeled and chopped
1 medium potato, peeled and chopped
1 leek, sliced and washed
1 clove garlic, crushed
1.7 litres stock
Seasoning
Freshly grated nutmeg

Prepare the cabbage by first cutting out any hard stalky bits or ribs and then shredding the leaves as thinly as possible. Now blanch the cabbage by placing it in a saucepan of cold water, bringing it to the boil and boiling for 1 minute, after which it needs to be drained in a colander. Next, using the same saucepan, heat the butter and fry the bacon until the fat starts to run from it. Add the onions, potato, leek and garlic, stir all the vegetables around and cook them until softened and slightly golden. Then stir in the drained cabbage and cook for another minute or two before pouring in the stock. Bring it back to the boil and then simmer very gently without a lid for about an hour. Finally taste and add seasoning and a little freshly grated nutmeg.

eggs
and us

Well, actually the egg and I are great
companions. I love them pure and

simple, as the advert says – in fact, I'm almost obsessed with them, forever
stopping the car on country roads and peeping over fences where the sign
says 'Eggs For Sale' just to see if the hens are running about, as my
grandmother puts it.

Alas, free-range is unrealistic nowadays, so mostly I make do with the
supermarket variety. Mind you, I'm just as obsessive there too, because fresh
certainly isn't unrealistic, and I'll always be grateful to the EEC for introducing
packing date-stamps on egg boxes. I no longer have to gaze and wonder
how long they've been hanging about: it tells you. I suppose, if you're in a
hurry, it can take a while to tot up which Week 34 is – but persevere, because
if we have to eat battery eggs, then at least they must be fresh.

Once you have a few fresh eggs in the house you'll never be short of a
quick cheap meal: there's something very reassuring about lightly boiled eggs
served with 'soldiers' of brown bread and butter, and freshly made tea.
However, in this chapter we're after something different – still the same good
old standby eggs but made into main meals that won't cost much extra (but
taste as if they did!).

*Thankfully we now have a choice: free-range eggs are available everywhere in
supermarkets, and battery eggs will have gone from the shelves in a few years' time.*

curried egg patties

This is good for an unexpected meal, provided you have half a dozen eggs in the house.

4 large hard-boiled eggs, chopped small
50g butter
40g plain flour
1 teaspoon Madras curry powder
1 teaspoon salt
150ml semi-skimmed milk
1 large egg, beaten
1 teaspoon tomato purée
1/2 teaspoon Worcestershire sauce
1/2 teaspoon lemon juice

To coat and cook:

Seasoned plain flour
1 large egg, beaten
Dried breadcrumbs
Oil for frying

Melt the butter in a saucepan, then stir in the flour, curry powder and salt. Cook for 2 minutes, then gradually stir in the milk to make a very thick sauce. Cook this for 5 minutes, stirring all the time, and then take the pan off the heat and add the beaten egg, tomato purée, Worcestershire sauce and lemon juice. Now add the hard-boiled eggs, stir to mix them in and season with salt. Next transfer the mixture to a bowl, cover and chill until the mixture becomes firm. Then before cooking form the mixture into 4 little round cakes, about 2cm thick, and dip them first in the seasoned flour, then in the beaten egg and finally in the breadcrumbs. Now shallow-fry them in 5mm of hot oil till golden brown and drain on kitchen paper before serving.

poached eggs with souffléed welsh rarebit

4 large, very fresh eggs for poaching
10g butter
10g plain flour
6 tablespoons semi-skimmed milk
$\frac{1}{2}$ teaspoon English mustard
A dash of Worcestershire sauce
A pinch of cayenne pepper
2 large eggs, separated
25g strong Cheddar cheese, grated
25g Parmesan cheese, grated
4 slices white bread (medium thick)
Seasoning

First heat some water in a frying pan with a little salt, ready to poach the eggs in. Then take a small saucepan, melt the butter in it, stir in the flour and cook over a medium heat for a minute or two before gradually stirring in the milk. Allow the mixture to bubble for 2 minutes, then take the saucepan off the heat and stir in the seasonings. Now beat the yolks of the 2 separated eggs, then stir them into the sauce and leave the mixture until it's cold. Next beat in the grated cheeses. Whisk the egg whites until they are stiff and carefully fold them into the cheese mixture. Now toast the bread on both sides and cover each slice thickly with the cheese mixture. Cook under a medium grill until the cheese mixture is puffed up and dark brown on top. During the last part – while you grill the cheese mixture – slip the 4 eggs into the simmering water in the frying pan to poach for 3 minutes. Lift them out with a draining spoon, resting it on kitchen paper to drain each egg, then pop one on each of the slices of toast.

eggs with cheese
and spinach sauce

Serves 2

This is very colourful to look at and quite filling when served with rice and a green salad.

225g fresh spinach leaves, cooked and drained, or 110g frozen spinach, thawed
4 large eggs
50g butter
1 small onion, peeled and finely chopped
25g plain flour
275ml semi-skimmed milk
75g Cheddar cheese, grated
2 tablespoons cream
Seasoning
Freshly grated nutmeg

Melt 40g of the butter in a small saucepan and gently soften the onion in it for 10 minutes. Then stir in the flour, cook for a minute or two and add the milk a little at a time, stirring after each addition, to make a smooth sauce. Taste and season the sauce, and let it cook for 6 minutes over a very gentle heat. Meanwhile boil the eggs by placing them in cold water, bringing them up to the boil and simmering them for 6 minutes, afterwards cooling them under cold running water. Now add two-thirds of the grated cheese to the sauce, stir it in and allow it to melt. Then transfer the sauce to a liquidiser, add the remaining 10g butter, the cream and the chopped drained spinach, and whizz the sauce until it's a pale green colour and only very tiny speckles of the spinach are visible. Season the sauce again, adding some nutmeg. Peel the eggs now, then halve them. Put a layer of sauce in a buttered oval 21cm gratin dish and arrange the eggs on top, rounded side up. Cover with the rest of the sauce, sprinkle with the remainder of the grated cheese and place the dish under a hot grill until the cheese is brown and the sauce is bubbling.

egg and bacon pie

I've always found the conventional egg and bacon pie a bit on the dry side, but this one is a whole lot nicer. Cold, it is very good for picnics.

For the filling:

4 large eggs
6 rashers lean streaky bacon, rinded
150ml semi-skimmed milk
Seasoning

For the shortcrust pastry:

175g plain flour
75g lard
A pinch each of salt and pepper
Cold water to mix

Preheat the oven to 200°C/400°F/gas mark 6 with a baking sheet in it.

First hard-boil 3 of the eggs by placing them in a saucepan, covering them with cold water, bringing it up to the boil and simmering gently for 7 minutes. Cool them rapidly under cold running water. Next either grill or fry the bacon rashers gently until the fat starts to run. While they're cooking, and the eggs are cooling, make the pastry (see page 230; if using ready-made pastry, the equivalent is 250g). Divide it in half, and use half to line an 18cm flan tin (if possible one with a 4cm-deep rim with sloping sides). Now peel and chop the hard-boiled eggs quite small, and chop the bacon fairly small as well. Next arrange the chopped bacon and eggs in the flan and season with freshly milled pepper and only a very little salt – because of the bacon. Now beat the remaining egg with the milk and pour it over the contents of the pie. Then roll out the rest of the pastry to make a lid, dampen the edges and seal well. Decorate with any trimmings, make a small hole in the centre and brush the top with milk. Bake on a highish shelf in the oven for 10 minutes, then reduce the heat to 180°C/350°F/gas mark 4 and bake for a further 30 minutes.

cheese soufflé

This is always a good standby recipe for using up old bits of cheese that are lurking in the bottom of the fridge.

75g cheese, grated
3 large eggs, separated
25g butter, plus a little extra
25g plain flour
150ml semi-skimmed milk
2 pinches of cayenne pepper
1/2 teaspoon mustard powder
Freshly grated nutmeg
Seasoning

Preheat the oven to 190°C/375°F/gas mark 5 with a baking sheet in it.

Butter an 1.5-litre soufflé dish well. Then take a medium-sized saucepan, melt 25g butter in it, add the flour and stir it over a medium heat for 2 minutes. Now add the milk gradually, stirring all the time till you have a smooth paste, and cook it very gently for 3 minutes (still stirring). Next stir in the seasonings, and allow the sauce to cool a bit before stirring in the grated cheese, followed by the egg yolks – which should be beaten quite thoroughly first. Now whisk the egg whites till they are stiff, beat a couple of dollops into the sauce, then fold the rest in very carefully and gently, so as not to lose all the air you've beaten into them. Pile the mixture into the soufflé dish next, then place it on a baking sheet in the centre of the oven for about 30–35 minutes.

To test if the soufflé is cooked, push a skewer down into the centre. If it comes out clean and the soufflé doesn't look too liquid, it's cooked.

cauliflower, egg and celery au gratin

This is a good one for vegetarians or anyone else who wants a delicious meal without any meat.

1 head English celery
1 cauliflower
110g mushrooms, sliced
2 large hard-boiled eggs, quartered
1 large onion, peeled and chopped
50g butter, plus a little extra
50g plain flour
275ml semi-skimmed milk
75g Cheddar cheese, grated
1 tablespoon dried breadcrumbs
1 bay leaf
1/4 whole nutmeg, grated
Seasoning
2 pinches of cayenne pepper

Preheat the oven to 220°C/425°F/gas mark 7.

Scrub and chop the celery into chunks and cook it in a little boiling salted water for about 20 minutes. The cauliflower needs to be trimmed, washed and sat in about 2.5cm of boiling salted water, together with the bay leaf, for about 10–15 minutes with the lid on the saucepan (both the celery and the cauliflower should be tender but still firm). When the cauliflower is ready, drain it – reserving the water – then separate it into small florets and arrange them in a buttered heatproof dish (25 x 16cm) along with the celery, sliced mushrooms and the quarters of hard-boiled egg. Now make the sauce by gently cooking the chopped onion in 50g of butter for about 10 minutes, then stirring in the flour and adding the milk bit by bit, stirring all the time. When all the milk is in, add 150–275ml of cauliflower water in the same way till you have a smooth sauce. Cook it gently for 6 minutes, then taste it and add seasoning and the grated nutmeg. Pour the sauce over the vegetables, sprinkle the grated cheese over, then the breadcrumbs, dot with flecks of butter and bake on a high shelf for 10 minutes until the cheese has browned and melted. Sprinkle with a couple of pinches of cayenne and serve hot.

poached eggs
with spinach soufflé

Serves 4

A very impressive way to serve eggs and spinach.

900g fresh spinach
4 large, very fresh eggs
50g butter, plus a little extra
Dry white breadcrumbs
50g plain flour
275ml semi-skimmed milk
50g cheese, grated
3 large egg yolks
4 large egg whites
Seasoning
Freshly grated nutmeg

Preheat the oven to 190°C/375°F/gas mark 5 with a baking sheet in it.

First liberally butter a 1.5-litre soufflé dish and dust the inside evenly with a few dry white breadcrumbs. Then thoroughly wash the spinach in several changes of cold water and pick it over, removing any thick, tough stalks or damaged leaves. Next press the leaves into a large saucepan, sprinkle with 2 teaspoons of salt (but don't add water), cover and cook for 7–10 minutes. Then drain the spinach thoroughly in a colander and chop it fairly finely. Now melt 50g butter in a medium-sized saucepan and stir in the flour. Cook for a minute or two before gradually stirring in the milk. Bring to boiling point and simmer, still stirring, for about 1 minute before removing the pan from the heat. Then beat the chopped spinach and two-thirds of the cheese into the mixture with the egg yolks. Now taste and add seasoning and a generous amount of nutmeg. At this stage poach the 4 eggs for 3 minutes in a frying pan of barely simmering water. While they are poaching, beat the egg whites till they are stiff, fold them carefully into the spinach mixture, then pour half the soufflé mixture into the dish. Add the poached eggs (well drained), cover with the rest of the soufflé mixture and sprinkle the top with the remaining cheese. Bake for 30–35 minutes, or until it is well risen and browned on top.

egg and anchovy salad

This is a nice dish for lunch on a hot summer's day with, maybe, a cold soup to start with.

6 large eggs
450g cooked new potatoes
110g cooked French beans (or sliced runner beans)
1 quantity of vinaigrette dressing (see page 148)
Seasoning

To finish:

1 lettuce, cleaned and prepared
1 x 50g tin anchovy fillets, well drained
25g black olives

Put the eggs in a saucepan, cover them with cold water, bring them up to a gentle simmer and cook for exactly 7 minutes. Then cool them rapidly under cold running water until they're quite cold. Now take the shells off and chop the eggs roughly, seasoning them lightly. Then slice the potatoes into rounds and cut the beans into 2.5cm lengths. Now take a large bowl, carefully mix the chopped eggs, beans and potatoes together, and pour in nearly all the vinaigrette dressing, keeping a little for later. Stir again, to get everything coated with the dressing, then cover the mixture and chill it until needed. To serve the salad, arrange the lettuce leaves in a salad bowl and sprinkle them with the reserved dressing. Then arrange the potato mixture over the lettuce, make a criss-cross pattern with the anchovies and finally sprinkle on the black olives.

potato and cheese baked eggs

This is a fairly economical supper dish that tastes especially good with home-made tomato sauce.

4 large, very fresh eggs
900g potatoes
75g butter, plus a little extra
150ml soured cream
175g Cheddar cheese, grated
Seasoning
A few chopped chives or spring onion tops

Preheat the oven to 190°C/375°F/gas mark 5.

Peel the potatoes, place them in a saucepan with some salt, pour boiling water on to them and cook them for about 25 minutes, or until tender. Then drain them, add 75g of butter and the soured cream, start to mash them with a fork and finish off by whipping them to a purée with an electric mixer. Now add the cheese, taste and season. Next butter a shallow ovenproof oval 21cm baking dish, arrange the potato mixture in the dish and, with the back of a tablespoon, make 4 evenly spaced depressions. Now break an egg carefully into each depression, place the dish in the oven and bake for 15 minutes, or until the eggs are just set. Serve sprinkled with chopped chives or spring onion tops.

eggs savoyard

For this recipe you could use 4 individual ovenproof bowls (about 275ml capacity), but failing that you can cook the whole lot in a large gratin dish.

4 large eggs
450g potatoes, peeled
50g butter
1 onion, peeled and finely chopped
8 tablespoons single cream
110g Cheddar cheese, grated
Seasoning

Preheat the oven to 200°C/400°F/gas mark 6.

First of all place the potatoes in a saucepan with some salt, pour in some boiling water and cook them for about 25 minutes. Then drain them, slice them (as you would for frying) and arrange an equal quantity in the base of each bowl. Next heat the butter in a saucepan and fry the onion until softened and golden. Then spoon a little of the melted butter and onion mixture over the sliced potatoes in each dish and season. Now make a slight depression in each bowl and carefully break in an egg. Next spoon 2 tablespoons of cream over each egg and season again with salt and pepper. Then sprinkle with cheese and bake in the oven for 15–20 minutes, or until hot and bubbling with the yolk still fairly soft. Serve absolutely immediately.

bacon, leek and potato omelette

This is a flat omelette, finished off under the grill, so it shouldn't be folded – just simply cut in half or in quarters.

4 large eggs
2 potatoes
1 leek
2 tablespoons oil
110g streaky bacon, rinded and diced
Seasoning
A generous pinch of Herbes de Provence

Peel and dice the potatoes and dry them on some kitchen paper, then trim the leek top and bottom. Slice it in half first lengthways and then across into 5mm thick strips, wash carefully in plenty of cold water, and drain and dry thoroughly. In a frying pan about 15cm in diameter heat the oil and add the diced potato. Cook gently for about 10 minutes, stirring frequently. When the potato is just tender, add the chopped leek and diced bacon to the pan. Stir well, cover with a suitably sized lid and cook over a low heat for a further 5–8 minutes. Meanwhile break the eggs into a bowl. Add seasoning and the Herbes de Provence. Stir to blend the eggs together, then pour the mixture over the contents of the pan. Shake the pan and cook over a low heat until the underside of the omelette is cooked and lightly golden. Meanwhile preheat the grill, then transfer the pan to the grill and continue to cook gently until the egg on the surface is just set. Cut the omelette in half or quarters and serve on warmed plates. This is nice with a crisp salad.

spanish tortilla

Serves 2

Tortilla, or Spanish omelette, can sometimes be just a mish-mash of leftovers incorporated in an omelette – but this is a real one made with green peppers and Spanish chorizo sausage.

4 large eggs
3 tablespoons oil
2 potatoes, peeled and diced
1 medium onion, peeled and chopped
1 small green pepper, deseeded and chopped
A 50g piece Spanish chorizo sausage, chopped small
Seasoning

For this you need a thick, heavy, medium-sized frying pan. Put 2 tablespoons of oil in it, then add the diced potatoes and cook them gently for about 8–10 minutes, stirring them around so that they brown evenly. Next add the onion, pepper and chorizo, stir again and continue cooking for a further 8–10 minutes, or until the potato and onion are soft. Now break the eggs into a bowl, season them well, beat them just a little bit with a fork, then pour them into the pan and, keeping the heat at medium, cook for 2 or 3 minutes, shaking the pan from time to time to prevent the eggs from sticking. When the omelette is firm but still slightly moist, slide it out on to a plate, then quickly heat the other tablespoon of oil in the pan and slide the omelette back in on its other side. Cook for another 3 minutes and serve cut in wedges.

omelettes piperade

Another quick supper dish, this is good towards the end of the summer when the tomatoes are plentiful and green peppers are cheap. For 2 omelettes the ingredients are:

4 large eggs
Oil
1 large green pepper, deseeded and chopped
1 onion, peeled and chopped
1 clove garlic, crushed
225g ripe tomatoes, skinned (see page 150) and chopped
1/2 teaspoon Herbes de Provence
Seasoning

Heat a little oil in a medium-sized pan, then stir in the chopped pepper, chopped onion and crushed garlic, and cook over a medium heat for about 5 minutes. Then add the tomatoes and Herbes de Provence, season and cook gently without a cover for about 20 minutes. Now get ready for the first omelette by breaking 2 eggs into a bowl, seasoning and stirring lightly with a fork. Then heat a smear of oil in an omelette pan and, when it is really hot, pour in the beaten egg and start to draw the eggs in to cook the omelette. After a few seconds, spoon half the pepper and tomato mixture over half the omelette, fold the other half of the omelette over the filling and invert the pan to tip the omelette out on to a warmed plate. Now quickly prepare the other omelette, using the remaining filling, and serve immediately with some crusty bread and a nice crisp green salad.

frugal fish

The funny thing is, frugal fish is usually the freshest. More expensive deep-sea fish, like cod and haddock, are very often three weeks old before they're landed – and (in my opinion) their dull flavour shows it. Since our home-caught herring and mackerel have far more character and flavour, I wonder why it's necessary to go off and fight wars over dull old cod?

But then we are a nation of fish-finger addicts, and once you've bitten your way through the bright orange breadcrumbs, what you've got is probably cod. We've already spoken of convenience versus cost but, quite honestly, fish fingers are outrageously expensive (I once reckoned up the price per pound of frozen fish fingers and discovered that in the same supermarket frozen rainbow trout was actually cheaper, and as it happens every bit as convenient but without the nasty breadcrumbs).

In this chapter I'm hoping to lure you on to a few very delicious recipes for herring and mackerel. I think it's a pity that because they were once less than a halfpenny each they've always had a poverty-stricken reputation. Well, when it comes to shopping for food we're all pretty poor now, so here's to their comeback! In the other recipes in this chapter I've attempted to make a little fish go a long way.

Also, when a recipe calls for white fish, do try the lesser-known varieties like pollack or red fish (sometimes called Norwegian cod), which are usually half the price of cod or haddock – and for any sort of fish pie, coley is very good.

Sorry about this. Now that not much 'dull' old cod is to be had I'm beginning to really appreciate it. We are into sustainable stocks and farmed fish nowadays, but herring and mackerel are still less expensive, wild and wonderful.

whiting au gratin

900g whiting fillets
25g butter, plus a little extra
1 onion, peeled, halved and thinly sliced
110g mushrooms, thinly sliced
1 teaspoon lemon juice
75ml dry cider
4 tablespoons dry white breadcrumbs
2 tablespoons grated cheese
Seasoning

Preheat the oven to 180°C/350°F/gas mark 4.

First heat 25g of butter in a saucepan and fry the onion gently until softened (about 10 minutes). Then stir in the mushrooms and lemon juice, and cook for about 3–4 minutes more. Season, then spread the mixture over the base of a buttered oval 21cm gratin dish. Lay the wiped whiting fillets on top and season again. Next pour in just enough cider to cover the mushroom/onion base. Finally sprinkle the breadcrumbs and cheese all over, dot with flecks of butter and bake – uncovered – on a high shelf in the oven for 25 minutes until golden brown and bubbling.

old-fashioned
soused herrings

Serves 3

Home-made rollmops beat anything that ever came out of a jar. You will need a shallow baking dish or casserole for this and also 6 toothpicks.

6 prepared herring fillets (with tails on if possible)*
6 teaspoons made mustard
2 dill pickles, sliced lengthways into 3
1 large onion, peeled and thinly sliced into rings
275ml cider vinegar
150ml dry cider
420ml water
3 juniper berries
3 allspice berries
2 cloves
8 peppercorns
1 bay leaf

Preheat the oven to 180°C/350°F/gas mark 4.

Check that all the herring bones have been removed and wipe the fillets as dry as possible with some kitchen paper. Now spread the filleted side of each fish with a teaspoon of mustard and place a slice of dill pickle across what was the head end of each fillet. Sprinkle the rest with some of the separated onion rings, roll up each fillet from the head end to the tail, being careful to get them as tight and neat as possible, and secure with a toothpick (through the tail end and out the other side). Now pack the rolls fairly tightly into the baking dish or casserole. Then prepare the marinade by placing the vinegar, cider and water in a saucepan, together with the spices and bay leaf. Bring the liquid to the boil and simmer (uncovered) for 10 minutes. Then take the pan from the heat and leave until the liquid is cold. To cook the herrings, pour the cold marinade over, cover with a lid or double sheet of foil and bake in the centre of the oven for 15 minutes. When they're cooked, let them get quite cold in the liquid, then cover them and put them in the refrigerator for at least 48 hours before serving. Serve, if possible, with rye bread.

✳ *If you do not have a fishmonger, prepared herring fillets can now be found in Morrisons, Waitrose and a number of other retailers.*

herrings fried in oatmeal

Just the thing for 'high tea' with some brown bread and butter and freshly made tea.

4 prepared herring fillets
50g lard
3 tablespoons medium oatmeal
Seasoning

Heat the lard in a large frying pan and, while it's heating, wipe the herrings with kitchen paper to get them as dry as possible. Season the oatmeal and then coat the herrings in it, pressing it down all over quite firmly. When the fat is hot and sizzling, fry the herrings for approximately 4 minutes on each side, until they're crisp and golden. Then drain them on crumpled kitchen paper and serve with wedges of lemon. Powdered mustard mixed with cream (or half-fat crème fraîche) goes very well with this dish and, instead of bread and butter, plain boiled potatoes.

baked fish soufflé

Whiting fillets, or fillets of any white fish, instantly become more special when made into a fluffy soufflé.

350g whiting fillets, cooked in 275ml semi-skimmed milk, then strained with the milk reserved
50g butter
40g plain flour
4 large egg yolks
2 tablespoons grated Parmesan cheese
2 teaspoons lemon juice
1 tablespoon finely chopped parsley
1 teaspoon anchovy essence or paste
3 spring onions, finely sliced
5 large egg whites
Salt and cayenne pepper

Preheat the oven to 200°C/400°F/gas mark 6.

Flake the fish, discarding the skin and bones as you go, then put it on one side while you make a sauce by melting the butter in a saucepan and stirring in the flour. Cook this for a minute or two before gradually adding the strained milk. Bring to the boil, stirring, and boil gently for 1 minute. Then remove the pan from the heat and beat in the egg yolks, 1 tablespoon of Parmesan cheese, the lemon juice, parsley, anchovy essence or paste, spring onions and the fish. Season well with salt and ½ teaspoon of cayenne pepper. Next whisk the egg whites to the stiff-peak stage. Then fold them into the fish mixture, taste and season again if necessary. Now pour the mixture into a buttered 1.7-litre soufflé dish or deep baking dish, and sprinkle with the remaining Parmesan cheese. Transfer the soufflé to the oven, placing it on a baking sheet, and turn down the heat immediately to 190°C/375°F/gas mark 5. Cook for 35–40 minutes, or until the soufflé is well risen and golden brown, then serve absolutely immediately.

baked fish with potatoes and anchovies

Any white fish can be used for this, because there's lots of flavour added.

450g white fish, skinned
450g potatoes, peeled and very thinly sliced
1 onion, peeled and finely chopped
6 tablespoons chopped parsley
1 clove garlic, crushed
Grated zest of 1 lemon
6 anchovy fillets, finely chopped
150ml semi-skimmed milk
25g butter
Seasoning

Preheat the oven to 180°C/350°F/gas mark 4.

Put a layer of potato slices in the base of a deepish, well-buttered baking dish and sprinkle with half the finely chopped onion. Then mix the parsley, garlic, lemon zest and finely chopped anchovy fillets together and sprinkle a little of this mixture in the dish before adding another layer of potatoes, some onion and another sprinkling of parsley mixture. Finish off with a final layer of potatoes (reserving a little of the parsley mixture). Now bring the milk up to the boil, season, then pour this over the potatoes, fleck the top with half the butter and bake (uncovered) for 40 minutes. Meanwhile cut the fish into smallish cubes; then after the 40 minutes is up, put the fish on top of the potatoes and sprinkle with the remaining parsley mixture and the remaining butter, and bake for a further 15–20 minutes, or until the fish is cooked.

mackerel en papillote

Cooking mackerel in paper cases keeps the flesh beautifully moist and tender.

2 prepared fresh mackerel
50g butter
4 tablespoons finely chopped parsley
1 small onion, peeled and grated
1 clove garlic, crushed
Juice of 1 lemon
1/4 teaspoon Herbes de Provence
A generous pinch of cayenne pepper
40g butter, melted
Seasoning

Preheat the oven to 200°C/400°F/gas mark 6.

Wipe the fish as dry as possible with kitchen paper, inside and out, and season. Then mix 50g of butter with the parsley, onion, garlic, lemon juice, Herbes de Provence and cayenne pepper and beat everything thoroughly to blend well. Then spread an equal quantity inside each fish. Now take two large circles of double-thickness greaseproof paper (each large enough to take a fish comfortably) and brush them with the melted butter. Then lay each fish in the middle on the buttered side, and wrap one side of the paper circle over the fish (to make a sort of Cornish pasty shape). Secure the edges by pinching them together, making small folds, then pop both parcels on to a baking sheet and bake for 30 minutes. Unwrap and serve with the juice from the packets poured over.

mackerel with rhubarb sauce

Not quite so famous as mackerel with gooseberries but just as good – the acidic fruit counteracts the richness of the fish perfectly.

2 prepared fresh mackerel
225g rhubarb
1 tablespoon demerara sugar
1/2 teaspoon ground ginger
150ml water
Seasoning

Make the sauce first by chopping the rhubarb into smallish chunks and putting it into a thick-based saucepan, adding the sugar, ginger and water. Then put a lid on and let it cook over a fairly gentle heat, shaking the saucepan from time to time. It will probably take around 15–20 minutes to soften. Now rub the contents of the saucepan through a sieve, or purée it in an electric blender, and taste to check that there is enough sugar (although it should be a fairly sharp sauce). Now preheat the grill, wipe the mackerel as dry as possible with kitchen paper, season the insides of the fish, then make three diagonal slashes across the backbone of each fish and grill them for about 4–6 minutes on each side. While they're grilling, reheat the sauce and serve it with the fish, together with new potatoes.

fishcakes with capers

Serves 4–6

A good way to make 450g of fish seem just like 900g.

450g mashed potatoes
450g poached cod (well drained)
2 tablespoons chopped parsley
3/4 teaspoon anchovy essence or paste
1 heaped teaspoon drained capers, chopped
1 large egg, beaten
25g butter
1 teaspoon lemon juice
Freshly grated nutmeg
1 clove garlic, crushed
Seasoning
A generous pinch of cayenne pepper

For the coating:
Plain flour
2 large eggs, beaten
175g (approx.) dry white breadcrumbs
Oil and butter for frying

In a large mixing bowl thoroughly combine everything except the seasoning, the cayenne pepper and the ingredients for the coating; then taste and season. (If the fish and potatoes are not freshly cooked and hot, the butter will need to be melted before adding it to the mixture.) Now cool and chill the mixture for an hour or two to get it nice and firm, then when you're ready to cook the fishcakes, lightly flour a working surface, turn the fish mixture out on to it and form it into a long roll about 5–6cm in diameter. Cut the roll into 12 round fishcakes. Pat each cake into a neat shape and dip it first into the beaten egg and then into the dry white breadcrumbs. Now shallow-fry the fishcakes in equal quantities of oil and butter until golden brown on both sides. Drain on crumpled kitchen paper and serve immediately. Tartare sauce or parsley sauce would be a nice accompaniment.

deep-fried sprats
with mustard sauce

Serves 2

In the good old days, when herrings were cheap and humble, their smaller cousins sprats were even humbler and it's only now that they're coming into their own again – which is a good thing, because they are delicious.

450g sprats
Seasoned plain flour
Groundnut oil for frying
2 pinches of cayenne pepper

For the mustard sauce:

25g butter
1/2 small onion, peeled and chopped
10g plain flour
2 teaspoons mustard powder
275ml semi-skimmed milk
Seasoning
2 teaspoons lemon juice
A generous pinch of sugar

Begin by making the mustard sauce. In a saucepan melt the butter and soften the chopped onion in it for about 10 minutes. Then stir in the flour and let it cook very gently for a couple of minutes before mixing in the mustard powder. Next add the milk bit by bit, stirring constantly. When all the milk is in, bring the sauce to the boil and let it simmer very gently for about 3 minutes. Then add seasoning, lemon juice and sugar to taste. Now keep the sauce warm while you gut and cook the sprats. Make a small incision behind a gill of each fish and gently squeeze the belly up towards the head to gut the fish, at the same time trying to leave the head intact. Then rinse the fish well and dry them thoroughly on some kitchen paper before tossing in seasoned flour. Next heat a deep pan of oil to 180°C/350°F, or, if you don't have a thermometer, until a small cube of bread dropped into it turns golden and crisp in 1 minute. Then fry the sprats in the oil for about 3 minutes. You will probably need to fry them in at least 2 batches. Then drain on crumpled kitchen paper, keeping them hot, and serve as soon as possible sprinkled with a trace of cayenne and with the mustard sauce poured over.

herrings with caper stuffing

4 prepared herring fillets
25g butter

For the stuffing:
75g fresh white breadcrumbs
1 teaspoon mustard powder
3 tablespoons finely chopped parsley
Grated zest of 1 lemon
Juice of ½ lemon
1 tablespoon drained capers, chopped
25g butter
1 medium onion, peeled and finely chopped
Seasoning

Preheat the oven to 220°C/425°F/gas mark 7.

To make the stuffing, first mix the breadcrumbs, mustard powder, parsley, lemon zest and juice, and capers together in a large mixing bowl. Now heat the butter in a frying pan and soften the onion in it for 10 minutes, before adding it (together with its buttery juices) to the breadcrumbs mixture and seasoning.

Now open each herring out flat and spread a quarter of the stuffing down one side of each one, then fold the other side back to its original shape. Put the fish in a well-buttered shallow baking dish (or else a roasting tin lined with foil), place a knob of butter on each one and bake near the top of the oven for 15 minutes, basting once with the buttery juices.

kipper quiche

A less frugal version of this can be made for a special occasion by substituting 275ml of double cream for the milk.

A pair of kippers (approx. 350g)
Shortcrust pastry (for amounts and method see page 230; if using ready-made, 275g)
A squeeze of lemon juice
275ml semi-skimmed milk
2 large eggs
2 teaspoons English mustard
Freshly grated nutmeg
Seasoning
A generous pinch of cayenne pepper

Preheat the oven to 180°C /350°F/gas mark 4 with a baking sheet in it.

Grill the kippers for a few minutes on each side, then set them aside to cool. Meanwhile make the pastry and line a 23–24cm fluted flan tin with it. Prick it all over the base with a fork and bake on the baking sheet near the top of the oven for 10 minutes, then remove the flan and increase the temperature of the oven to 190°C/375°F/gas mark 5. Next carefully skin the fish, separate the flesh into large flakes, lay these over the base of the pastry case and squeeze a little lemon juice over the top. Now whisk the milk, eggs, mustard and freshly grated nutmeg together with some seasoning. Place the flan on the heated baking sheet in the centre of the oven, pour the liquid mixture carefully into it and sprinkle with cayenne pepper. Then bake for about 40 minutes until the filling is slightly puffed and golden. Served hot, warm or cold, it is delicious.

salmon fishcakes

Serves 3

I think tinned salmon makes very good fishcakes, as nice as if you'd used fresh.

1 x 210g tin salmon
225g potatoes, peeled
2 tablespoons chopped parsley
2 gherkins, finely chopped
2 large hard-boiled eggs, chopped
2 teaspoons lemon juice
1 teaspoon anchovy essence or paste
Plain flour
Oil and butter for frying
Seasoning
A generous pinch of cayenne pepper

Begin by boiling the potatoes in salted water, then drain and mash them. Meanwhile drain the liquor from the salmon, discarding any skin or bones, and mash it to a paste with a fork. Then combine the potato with the fish, parsley, gherkins, hard-boiled egg, lemon juice and anchovy essence or paste. Mix everything thoroughly, taste and add seasoning and cayenne pepper. Next form the mixture into 6 fishcakes and dust each one with flour (all this can be done in advance). Then fry the fishcakes in equal quantities of hot oil and butter on both sides until golden. Drain and serve hot, garnished with sprigs of parsley and wedges of lemon.

cold marinated mackerel

Serves 2

This makes a lovely summer dish to serve on a very hot day with, perhaps, some rice salad to accompany it.

2 prepared fresh mackerel

225g ripe tomatoes, skinned (see page 150), deseeded and chopped

1 small green pepper, deseeded and finely chopped

1 small onion, peeled and finely chopped

1/2 small lemon, thinly sliced

150ml dry cider

3 tablespoons cider vinegar

4 tablespoons oil

1/2 teaspoon Herbes de Provence

Seasoning

2 pinches of cayenne pepper

2 tablespoons chopped parsley

Wipe the fish clean with kitchen paper, then arrange them in an oval fireproof casserole just large enough to hold them side by side – alternatively, you could fit them into a frying pan. Now place the rest of the ingredients (except the seasonings and parsley) in a saucepan, cover and simmer for 20 minutes. Taste and add seasoning and a couple of pinches of cayenne pepper, then pour the mixture over the fish in the casserole. Now bring it up to the boil and simmer very gently for just 5 minutes. Turn the fish over very carefully, cover again and leave them to become quite cold in the juices in the casserole. Serve sprinkled with chopped parsley.

mackerel with caper sauce

2 prepared fresh mackerel
5 tablespoons oil
1 large clove garlic, crushed
Juice of 1 large lemon
110g drained capers, chopped
Seasoning

A few hours before you need to cook the fish, put the oil in a bowl with the crushed garlic and beat in the lemon juice, followed by the capers and some seasoning. Then leave it on one side for the flavours to develop. When you are ready to cook the fish, remove the grill rack from the grill and line it with foil. Preheat the grill and arrange the fish on the foil, after gashing each side of the fish twice (in the thickest part of their bodies). Season, then pour the caper sauce in and around the fish. Brush a little oil over each one. Grill under a high heat so that the skins turn crisply brown – they will need 3–4 minutes on each side. Then serve with all the pan juices poured over. You'll need lots of crusty bread to mop them up.

tomato and anchovy quiche

This has a lovely Mediterranean flavour and tastes very good eaten out of doors on a hot summer's day.

Shortcrust pastry (for amounts and method see page 230; if using ready-made, 250g)
1 tablespoon olive oil
2 medium onions, peeled and finely chopped
1 clove garlic, crushed
700g tomatoes, skinned (see page 150), deseeded and chopped
1 teaspoon Herbes de Provence
1 x 50g tin anchovy fillets
3 tablespoons tomato purée
2 tablespoons chopped parsley
2 large eggs
25g black olives, pitted and halved
2 tablespoons grated Parmesan cheese
Seasoning

Preheat the oven to 180°C/350°F/gas mark 4 with a baking sheet in it.

Begin by lining a 25.5cm flan tin with the pastry, prick the base all over with a fork and bake it for 15 minutes. Then remove it from the oven and increase the heat to 190°C/375°F/gas mark 5. Meanwhile heat the oil in a medium-sized saucepan and cook the finely chopped onions and crushed garlic over a gentle heat until softened but not coloured. Then stir in the chopped tomatoes and Herbes de Provence, and cook, uncovered, over a fairly high heat until the mixture is reduced to a thick consistency and most of the excess liquid has evaporated. Now drain the anchovies, retaining the oil from the tin. Chop up 6 anchovies, then cut the rest in half lengthways and keep them on one side. Remove the pan from the heat and stir in the 6 chopped fillets, tomato purée and parsley; then beat the eggs together in a basin before stirring them into the tomato mixture. Taste and season if necessary. Now spread the mixture evenly in the flan case and decorate the top with a lattice-work of the remaining halved anchovy fillets. Scatter over the olives, then sprinkle the surface with the oil retained from the anchovy tin and finally with the Parmesan cheese. Now bake for 40 minutes until the filling is puffed and light brown.

chickens' lib

Chicken is a problem. The cheapest form is the frozen variety, and most

chickens sold in this country are frozen. Being only seven to eight weeks old, they are also tasteless, and have probably been fed on fish protein (which has an alarming knack of impregnating a bird with a fishy flavour if not removed from the diet a month before the bird is killed). On the other hand, the best chicken to buy is the one that has been allowed to hang in the family butcher's and is drawn only at the point of purchase, but that is also the most expensive.

It's not quite as straightforward as that, though. Very many frozen chickens that come off the production line are eviscerated quickly, then plunged into a trough of iced water to be cooled rapidly. At the same time they absorb up to 10 per cent of their own weight in water and then are packed off to be frozen, water and all. You are in effect paying for 10 per cent water when you buy many frozen chickens.

Fortunately, there is an alternative to water-cooling and that is air-cooling, in which no water is absorbed to increase weight or extract flavour. That is why supermarket, fresh-chilled chickens don't have the bleached white look which so many mass-produced varieties have: they have that healthy pinkish tinge you find on fresh chickens hanging in the butcher's.

In short, if you can't get hold of a freshly drawn bird from a butcher, my advice is to plump for an air-chilled chicken – and in the interests of frugality, go back to the days when chicken was a treat by having fewer but better-flavoured ones.

Some improvements over the years, I suppose. Fish meal has gone, as has water-cooling, and battery chickens will be subject to an EU ban by 2012. However, the very best chicken, aged, well hung and sold including giblets, is still a rarity.

chicken pot roast

Serves 4–6

Needless to say you'll need a freshly drawn chicken for this, and ask your supplier to be sure to give you the giblets.

A 1.6kg roasting chicken
Butter
1 largish onion, peeled and stuck with 3 cloves
4 leeks, trimmed and washed
4 carrots, scraped
4 sticks celery, halved
A few parsley stalks
1 bay leaf
1 clove garlic, crushed
Seasoning
2 tablespoons chopped parsley

Preheat the oven to 230°C/450°F/gas mark 8.

First rub the inside of the chicken with seasoning and a little butter. Then place the onion stuck with cloves inside the chicken and rub some butter and seasoning over the outside. Now put the chicken in a roasting tin and bake in the top half of the oven for about 30 minutes, by which time it should have developed a nice golden-brown skin. Then remove it from the oven and transfer it, together with any juices, to a deep pot. Surround the chicken with the vegetables, herbs and garlic, and pour over sufficient water to not quite cover the bird, adding the giblets as well. Bring to boiling point and simmer very gently with the lid on for about 1 hour, or until the chicken is tender, then remove the chicken and vegetables and keep warm. Now discard the giblets and boil the remaining stock briskly until it has reduced and the flavour has concentrated. Carve the chicken on to a serving dish, add the vegetables, spoon some of the juices over, sprinkle with chopped parsley and serve. Any stock left over can be used for soup.

poulet à la catalane

This is a good recipe if you're looking for an inexpensive dish for a special occasion, especially in the autumn, when peppers and aubergines are at their cheapest.

A 1.6–1.8kg chicken, cut into 6 joints
50g butter
Olive oil
2 medium onions, peeled and chopped
1 clove garlic, crushed
225ml dry cider
1 sprig fresh thyme
1 bay leaf
3 small aubergines, cut into 2.5cm cubes
2 medium green peppers, deseeded and sliced
6 tomatoes, skinned (see page 150) and chopped
110g mushrooms, sliced
110g Spanish stuffed olives, sliced
Seasoning

Preheat the oven to 190°C/375°F/gas mark 5.

In a large flameproof casserole heat the butter and 2 tablespoons of olive oil together. Season the chicken joints and cook them to a nice golden brown, turning them over in the hot fat, then add the onions and the crushed garlic. Stir them around and let them cook for about 5–7 minutes. Now pour in the cider, let it bubble for a minute or two, add the thyme and bay leaf, then put the lid on and place the casserole in the oven to cook for about 45 minutes. Towards the end of that time, heat a little more oil in a frying pan and gently cook the chopped aubergines, peppers, tomatoes and mushrooms till soft, seasoning well. When the chicken is ready, take the casserole out of the oven, add all the vegetables plus the sliced olives and simmer the whole lot on top of the stove for about 5 minutes. Then spoon off any surplus fat, extract the thyme and bay leaf, and serve the chicken on a warmed serving dish, garnished if you like with little triangular croutons of crisp-fried bread.

devilled chicken drumsticks

Serves 3

Supermarkets and good butchers do very reasonably priced packets of chicken drumsticks.

6 chicken drumsticks
2 tablespoons Worcestershire sauce
1 tablespoon tomato purée
1 tablespoon tomato ketchup
2 teaspoons made mustard
1 teaspoon sugar
1 teaspoon soy sauce
1 teaspoon paprika
1 tablespoon oil
Seasoning

Start by arranging the chicken drumsticks in a single layer in the grill pan with the grid removed; then, using a skewer, stab the joints in several places. Now in a mixing bowl combine all the remaining ingredients together and stir thoroughly until smooth. Pour this mixture over the chicken and turn the pieces around in it. Then leave it, covered with foil, in a cool place for a minimum of 3 hours – or much longer if you like.

To cook, preheat the grill, then grill the chicken for about 15–20 minutes, or until the drumsticks are cooked. Keep turning them fairly frequently, to prevent them burning, and serve very hot with any pan juices spooned over. Onion rice (see page 166) is nice with this.

chicken and chickpeas

Serves 4

Chickpeas give an unusual flavour to a chicken casserole as well as making it more substantial.

A 1.15–1.35kg roasting chicken, quartered
225g chickpeas, soaked overnight and drained
25g butter
2 tablespoons oil
1 large onion, peeled, halved and sliced
2 cloves garlic, crushed
1 x 400g tin Italian tomatoes
275ml stock (made from the giblets)
1 bay leaf
1–2 tablespoons tomato purée
1 teaspoon Herbes de Provence
Seasoning

Preheat the oven to 170°C/325°F/gas mark 3.

Place the chickpeas in a saucepan with enough fresh water to cover them to a depth of about 5cm, then bring to the boil. Do not add any salt at this stage. Simmer (uncovered) for about 30 minutes, skimming after about 10 minutes. While that's happening, heat the butter and oil together in a flameproof casserole, then dry the chicken quarters on kitchen paper and fry in the hot fat over a medium heat until they're evenly browned. Using a draining spoon, remove them to a plate and in the fat remaining in the pan gently fry the sliced onion and crushed garlic until softened. Now return the chicken to the pan and pour over the tomatoes and stock. Then drain the cooked chickpeas, reserving their cooking liquor. Add them to the chicken mixture with 150ml of the liquor as well. Next add the bay leaf, tomato purée and Herbes de Provence, and season. Bring up to simmering point, cover and transfer the casserole to the oven. Bake for 30 minutes, then remove the lid and bake for a further 30 minutes. Taste and add a bit more seasoning if necessary before serving. Onion Rice (see page 166) is nice with this.

southern fried chicken

I use the packets of chicken thighs or drumsticks for this, but you could use a 1.35kg chicken cut into 8 pieces.

8 chicken joints
Groundnut oil for deep-frying
A little semi-skimmed milk
110g plain flour
1/2 teaspoon baking powder
Seasoning
Rock salt, crushed

Into a wide, deep pan pour enough oil to give a depth of 2.5cm and heat to 180°C/350°F, or until a small cube of bread turns crisp and golden in 1 minute. Meanwhile, dip the chicken pieces in milk. Mix the flour with the baking powder (I use a plastic bag), and season well. Jump the chicken joints up and down in the flour to coat them evenly. Now deep-fry them in the oil for 15 minutes, turning them over occasionally. When the chicken joints are cooked, drain them on crumpled kitchen paper and serve immediately, sprinkled with a little crushed rock salt.

In America, Southern Fried Chicken has a traditional accompaniment of fried bananas and corn fritters. I think it's equally nice with some sauté potatoes and a crisp salad.

spiced chicken pilau

Not all Indian dishes are as long and as complicated as you would imagine. This one, for instance, can be made very easily at home.

A 1.1–1.35kg roasting chicken, cut into 8 joints (plus giblets)
2 tablespoons groundnut oil
2 medium onions, peeled and finely chopped
1 green pepper, deseeded and finely chopped
2 cloves garlic, crushed
1 heaped teaspoon ground ginger
1 teaspoon turmeric
1 teaspoon Madras curry powder
2.5cm cinnamon stick
150ml natural yoghurt
275ml long-grain rice
570ml chicken stock made with the giblets
2 bay leaves, crumbled
2 cloves
Seasoning

Wipe the chicken joints and season them. Heat the oil in a large saucepan or flameproof casserole and fry them until well browned. Then, using a draining spoon, remove the chicken to a plate and gently fry the chopped onions, pepper and garlic in the fat remaining in the pan. As soon as they're softened (about 6 minutes), stir in the ginger, turmeric, curry powder and cinnamon, then return the chicken joints to the pan and stir in the yoghurt. Cover the pan and cook gently for about 15 minutes, giving it a shake from time to time. Now uncover the pan and stir in the rice, followed by the stock, bay leaves and cloves. Then bring to simmering point, cover and cook gently for about 20 minutes. After that remove the pan from the heat and leave (covered) until the rice has absorbed the excess liquid. Now taste and season, if it needs it, and serve with some mango chutney.

mustard-coated chicken

Serves 4

It's best to prepare this 3–4 hours in advance so that the mustard flavours can penetrate the chicken.

8 small chicken joints (wings and thighs), or a whole chicken cut into 8 pieces
2 tablespoons made mustard
1 tablespoon Dijon mustard
2 large eggs
150g dry white breadcrumbs
Plain flour
Groundnut oil for deep-frying
Seasoning

Begin by removing the skins from the chicken joints, then in a small basin blend together smoothly both mustards and the eggs. Now take 2 squares of greaseproof paper: on one place the breadcrumbs and on the other some flour. Season each chicken joint and dust with flour. Then dip each one into the mustard mixture (making sure it's evenly coated) and roll it in the breadcrumbs, patting the crumbs on firmly. Place all the joints on a large plate and chill for 3–4 hours.

To cook the chicken you'll need either a very large frying pan or two smaller ones with about 2.5cm of oil, heated to the stage where a small cube of bread froths on contact. Fry the chicken joints over a medium heat for about 20 minutes in all, turning them over occasionally – they should be crisp and golden. Drain on crumpled kitchen paper and serve hot.

spiced chicken
with lentils

Serves 6

For this recipe try to buy the whole brown or green lentils, and don't worry if
you haven't got all the relevant spices, you can use curry powder instead – about
2 teaspoons of the hot Madras kind.

A 1.6kg chicken, cut into 6 portions
2 tablespoons groundnut oil
2 medium onions, peeled and sliced
1 clove garlic, crushed
1 heaped teaspoon ground coriander
1 teaspoon ground ginger
1 teaspoon ground cumin
1 teaspoon turmeric
1/2–3/4 teaspoon chilli powder (depending on how hot you like it)
225g whole lentils, soaked in cold water for half an hour
1 tablespoon tomato purée
425ml chicken stock made with the giblets
Salt

Preheat the oven to 180°C/350°F/gas mark 4.

Start by heating the oil in a flameproof casserole and fry the chicken portions
to a nice golden colour all over. Then set them on one side and add the onions
and garlic to the pan. Soften them for about 5 minutes, then stir in the spices and
cook for another 5 minutes. Now return the chicken pieces to the casserole and
spoon the spicy onion and oil mixture over them. Next add the drained lentils,
then mix the tomato purée with the hot chicken stock and pour that in. Now add
a little salt and bring everything up to simmering point – and make sure all the
lentils are pushed down so that they are almost covered by the liquid. Put a lid on
and transfer the casserole to the oven, where it will take about 45 minutes to an
hour to cook. Serve with rice and mango chutney.

forequarter
front

The figures are well known: it takes 4.5kg of grain to get 450g of beef.

About 40–50 per cent of our beef is grain-fed, therefore each time there is a bad harvest world grain prices rocket (and so do beef prices). You don't have to be a monetary expert to see that it's a very wasteful way of intensively producing protein.

I don't think we should do without beef altogether, but as the world population increases – and grain shortages along with it – it would be unrealistic to think of the future of meat as anything but doubtful. Textured Vegetable Protein (TVP, see page 195) has now arrived and laboratory nutritionists are already investigating such phenomena as 'bacterial' proteins. As for us, well perhaps the affluent era of everyday steaks, chops and grills is on the way out, but by world standards we still have a lot of meat in this country. However, because it's going to cost us more and more, I feel that from now on we have to make the best possible use of it.

There's no such thing as a cheap cut any more, but forequarter meat (on me that's from the waist up) is less expensive and does get overlooked, since it needs more careful and longer cooking. Yet if you're prepared to take the trouble, forequarter meat very often has a far better flavour.

I promise that if you were to make a direct comparison you would find that shoulder of lamb has a sweeter flavour than leg; similarly, belly and shoulder of pork compared with leg. And silverside and topside are mere shadows of chuck when it comes to pot-roasting or braising. Flavour is not a feature of intensively reared meat at the best of times, so let us nurture what little we have (lamb being the one exception, of course – the only reliable species of 'free-range' meat left to us). So forward forequarters, as in the following recipes, which may take a little longer to cook but won't be difficult to prepare.

✳ *Thankfully I can report that TVP did not catch on! The good news is that farmers are returning more and more to traditional outdoor rearing, but with the same grain crisis facing us we need more than ever to make use of forequarter meat.*

braised pork with prunes

700g lean belly of pork or spare ribs, cut into cubes

1 dessertspoon oil

6 juniper berries, crushed

1/2 teaspoon chopped thyme (fresh or dried)

225g onions, peeled and sliced

1 clove garlic, crushed

110g prunes, halved and pitted

1 large cooking apple, peeled, cored and sliced

A little caster sugar

700g potatoes, peeled and thickly sliced

A little butter

150ml dry cider

Seasoning

Preheat the oven to 170°C/325°F/gas mark 3.

Fry the pork in the oil to brown it nicely, then arrange it in the bottom of a shallow (and fairly wide) fireproof casserole or pie dish. Season and sprinkle over the crushed juniper berries and the chopped thyme. Now fry the onions and garlic in the same frying pan for a little while, then put them round the pork with a few pieces of prune tucked here and there. Next arrange the apple slices all over and give them a very slight dusting of caster sugar. Finally, arrange the thick potato slices on top, making them overlap one another. Season again, then dot with a few flecks of butter and pour in the cider. Cover and bake for 1½ hours. When the cooking time's up, raise the heat to 230°C/450°F/gas mark 8, remove the lid and cook for a further 20 minutes or so, until the potatoes have turned a lovely golden brown (or brown them under a hot grill).

roast lamb with coriander

In the winter, when only imported lamb is reasonably priced, this is a good way to jazz up half a shoulder.

½ shoulder of lamb
1 clove garlic, cut into slivers
1 tablespoon coriander seeds
Stock or dry cider

Preheat the oven to 190°C/375°F/gas mark 5.

Place the meat in a roasting tin and, using a small sharp knife, make about 6–8 evenly placed incisions in it. Into these slits push slivers of garlic and the coriander seeds (crushed a bit first, using either a pestle and mortar or the back of a tablespoon). Roast for 30 minutes per 450g, basting with the juices from time to time. When the lamb is cooked, carve it into thick slices and keep warm. Then strain off the fat from the roasting tin and add a little stock or dry cider to the juices to make a gravy. Redcurrant jelly is a nice accompaniment.

beef in cider

This is an inexpensive dish, although special enough for a dinner party – quite simply a classic boeuf bourguignon only made with cider and every bit as good.

900g chuck steak, cut into largish chunks
1 tablespoon oil
1 medium onion, peeled and sliced
1 rounded tablespoon plain flour
420ml dry cider
2 cloves garlic, chopped
2 sprigs fresh thyme (or ½ teaspoon dried)
1 bay leaf
350g small onions or shallots, peeled and left whole
225g streaky bacon in one piece (or use lardons)
110g dark flat mushrooms, sliced
Seasoning

Preheat the oven to 150°C/300°F/gas mark 2.

Start off by heating half the oil in a very large solid frying pan and frying the sliced onion for 5 minutes. Then turn the heat right up, add the cubes of meat and brown them quickly on all sides, tossing them around frequently. Next sprinkle in the flour, stir it around to soak up all the juices, then gradually pour in the cider – stirring all the time – and add the chopped garlic and herbs. Season, then pour the whole lot into a casserole, put a lid on and cook in the oven for 2 hours. Now, using the rest of the oil, fry the small onions and bacon to colour them lightly, and add them to the casserole together with the sliced mushrooms. Then put the lid back on and cook for a further hour. This is nice served with Onion Rice or buttered noodles (see pages 166 or 169).

pork and kidney hotpot

Serves 3–4

I love to use juniper berries with pork dishes, but if you haven't got – or can't get
– any, just leave them out.

450g lean belly of pork, cut into cubes
1 dessertspoon oil
2 tablespoons well-seasoned plain flour
1 pork kidney, trimmed and sliced
1/2 teaspoon dried sage
6 juniper berries, crushed
1 largish onion, peeled and chopped
1 clove garlic, crushed
1 medium cooking apple, peeled and thinly sliced
275ml stock or dry cider
900g potatoes, peeled and thickly sliced
A little melted butter
Seasoning

Preheat the oven to 190°C/375°F/gas mark 5.

Heat the oil in a largish frying pan, then dust the pieces of pork in seasoned
flour and fry them to a nice golden brown all round. Now, using a draining spoon,
transfer them to a pie dish (I use an old pie dish of about 1.5 litres capacity). Next
fry the slices of kidney (which should also have been dipped in seasoned flour)
and tuck those in among the pork; then sprinkle the sage and crushed juniper
berries over the pork, followed by some seasoning. Now soften the onion and
garlic in the frying pan for about 10 minutes, then sprinkle them over the meat,
followed by the slices of apple. Next pour in the stock or cider and finally top
everything with the slices of potato overlapping each other. Season the potatoes,
brush them with a little melted butter and bake the hotpot in the oven for about
1 hour, or until the potatoes are golden brown and the pork is tender.

baked stuffed
breast of lamb

1 large breast of lamb, boned (approx. 350–400g)

For the stuffing:
50g fresh breadcrumbs
1 medium onion, peeled and very finely chopped
1 tablespoon chopped parsley
1 tablespoon chopped mint
1 teaspoon finely chopped rosemary
¼ whole nutmeg, grated
Grated zest of ½ lemon
1 large egg, beaten
Seasoning

Preheat the oven to 180°C/350°F/gas mark 4.

In a mixing bowl, mix the breadcrumbs, onion, parsley, mint and rosemary, then add the nutmeg and lemon zest. Mix thoroughly and season well. Now stir in the beaten egg to bind the stuffing together, then spread the stuffing evenly over the breast of lamb and roll the lamb up gently and not too tightly. Tuck the flap end over and tie the meat in 3 places with string – again not too tightly. Press back any bits of stuffing that fall out, wrap the meat in foil, place it in a roasting tin and bake for 1½ hours. Then unwrap the foil, baste with the juices and brown for a further 30 minutes, basting again once or twice. Serve the meat cut in thick slices with thin gravy made with the juices, and some redcurrant jelly.

pork rissoles with spiced apple sauce

These are lovely served with creamy mashed potatoes.

450g shoulder of pork, cut into chunks
1 onion, peeled and quartered
110g stale bread
1 cooking apple, peeled, cored and quartered
1 tablespoon chopped sage
1/4 teaspoon ground mace
1 teaspoon salt
Freshly milled black pepper

For the sauce:
1/2 small onion, peeled and chopped
25g butter
225g cooking apples, peeled and chopped
1 tablespoon water
Freshly grated nutmeg
2 pinches of ground cloves
Sugar to taste

Preheat the oven to 190°C/375°F/gas mark 5.

Chop the pork, onion, bread and apple in a processor and mix them thoroughly with the remaining rissole ingredients. Form the mixture into balls and arrange in the base of a small buttered roasting tin. Cover with some buttered foil and bake in the top half of the oven for 45 minutes. Then remove the foil, raise the oven temperature to 200°C/400°F/gas mark 6 and continue to bake for a further 30 minutes, basting every so often, until the rissoles are nicely browned on top. Meanwhile, to make the sauce, soften the onion in the butter for 10 minutes, then stir in the chopped apple and the water. Cover and simmer till soft, before adding the nutmeg, cloves and sugar. Beat the sauce till it's fluffy and serve hot with the rissoles.

shoulder of lamb stuffed with rice and olives

1.35–2.25kg shoulder of lamb, boned

¼ teaspoon finely chopped rosemary

75–110g minced lamb

1 clove garlic, crushed

75ml rice, cooked (that's 75ml weight before cooking)

50g chopped onion

12 Spanish stuffed olives (6 of them quartered or sliced for the stuffing)

2 tablespoons chopped parsley

1 large egg, beaten

Seasoning

For the gravy:

20g plain flour

275ml stock

Preheat the oven to 200°C/400°F/gas mark 6.

Begin by seasoning the inside surfaces of the meat and sprinkling over the rosemary. Then mix the minced lamb with the crushed garlic, cooked rice, chopped onion, chopped olives, parsley and a little of the beaten egg. Spread the stuffing over the meat, then roll the meat up as neatly as possible into a cylindrical shape. Now tie loops of string round it at 5cm intervals, and season the surface. Next place the meat in a roasting tin and roast for 25 minutes per 450g. When it's cooked, remove the string and place it on a warmed serving dish to keep warm while you make the gravy. Using the juices in the pan, stir in the flour, then add the stock bit by bit, followed by the whole olives. Serve the meat with the gravy separate – and some new carrots and new potatoes would be a nice accompaniment.

pot roast of pork with cabbage and juniper

1.35kg shoulder of pork, boned and rolled
570g white cabbage
3 tablespoons oil
2 medium onions, peeled and sliced
1 clove garlic, sliced
2 carrots, scraped and sliced
¼ teaspoon dried thyme (or a sprig of fresh)
12 juniper berries, crushed
Seasoning
A little chopped parsley

Preheat the oven to 160°C/325°F/gas mark 3.

Wipe the joint as dry as possible, then heat the oil in an extra large flameproof casserole and, with the heat fairly high, brown the pork steadily all over. Then remove it to a plate while you fry the sliced onions, garlic and carrots for about 10 minutes or so. Now replace the joint in the casserole and bring it up to sizzling point. Season it and sprinkle with the dried thyme and the juniper berries, then put a lid on and transfer it to the oven to bake for 1 hour, giving it a basting with the juices about halfway through the cooking time. Meanwhile slice the cabbage. Bring a large saucepan of salted water to the boil, add the sliced cabbage, bring back to the boil and cook for 3 minutes, then rinse in cold water and drain in a colander, pressing out any excess liquid. When the hour is up, remove the casserole from the oven, add the drained cabbage and stir it into the juices in the casserole. Now reheat until bubbling, cover again and replace in the oven for a further hour (once more basting the joint midway). When the time's up, remove the joint and slice into serving pieces, then taste and season the cabbage mixture. Arrange the sliced pork over the cabbage, sprinkle with chopped parsley and serve with some crunchy roast potatoes.

pork with summer vegetables

Because lamb is so popular during the summer months, pork is very often down in price. (Let's hope!)

2 spare rib chops
1 dessertspoon oil
1/2 teaspoon chopped rosemary
6 shallots or small onions, peeled and left whole
4 small or 2 large new carrots, scraped and sliced
150ml boiling water
350g fresh peas (weighed in the pods)
Seasoning

Preheat the oven to 170°C/325°F/gas mark 3.

First heat the oil in a frying pan and brown the chops, colouring them a nice golden brown on both sides. Then transfer them to a large ovenproof dish (I use a 1.7-litre oval pie dish) and sprinkle them with the rosemary. Now add the whole shallots and the sliced carrots to the pan, and cook to colour them a little too. Then, using a draining spoon, arrange them round the pork, season and pour in 150ml of boiling water. Cover the dish with a double sheet of foil (or a lid) and transfer to the oven for an hour. Meanwhile shell the peas. When the hour is up, stir the peas down into the juices, taste and add a little more seasoning if necessary; then re-cover with the foil and cook for an extra 20–30 minutes, depending on the age of the peas. Serve with new potatoes tossed in butter and snipped chives.

NOTE: *If you can't get any shallots or small onions, use a couple of ordinary-sized ones, sliced.*

mutton pot pie

Serves 4

The bones in the meat give this a delicious sauce, while the suet crust on top makes it very filling and substantial – in fact, don't plan to do anything much for a while after eating it.*

8 large pieces middle neck of lamb
2 tablespoons seasoned plain flour
1 clove garlic, crushed
1 teaspoon Herbes de Provence
2 medium onions, peeled and chopped
3 medium carrots, scraped and sliced
450g potatoes, peeled and sliced
2 tablespoons pearl barley
Seasoning

For the suet-crust pastry:
225g self-raising flour
110g shredded suet

Preheat the oven to 150°C/300°F/gas mark 2.

Trim any excess fat from the lamb, then dust the pieces with seasoned flour and arrange a layer of meat in the bottom of a heavy flameproof casserole, about 2.25 litres capacity, followed by a sprinkling of the crushed garlic and Herbes de Provence, then a layer of vegetables and a tablespoon of pearl barley. Season well. Repeat the layers and finally add enough boiling water to almost cover everything. Then put on the lid and cook in the oven for about 2 hours. Just before the end of the cooking time, make the pastry by mixing the flour and suet with some seasoning and just enough cold water to make a smooth, elastic dough. Now remove the casserole and turn the heat right up to 220°C/425°F/gas mark 7. Roll the pastry out to a round big enough to just fit inside the rim of the casserole. Put it on and make a small hole in the centre. Return the casserole to the oven (without a lid this time) and let the pastry cook for 30 minutes. Serve immediately.

 Can't face making a suet crust? Leave it out and simply serve this as a stew.

brown beef stew
with dumplings

450g of chuck steak will serve 4 easily in this recipe, which includes plenty of vegetables and some fluffy dumplings.

450g chuck steak, cubed
50g beef dripping
4 smallish onions, peeled and left whole
1 medium turnip, peeled and cut into chunks
1/2 swede, peeled and cut into chunks
6 small carrots, scraped and left whole
A knob of butter
1 1/2 tablespoons plain flour
570ml boiling water
1 bay leaf
1/2 teaspoon Herbes de Provence
1 1/2 teaspoons Worcestershire sauce
Seasoning

For the dumplings:
110g self-raising flour
50g shredded suet
1 tablespoon chopped parsley

Preheat the oven to 150°C/300°F/gas mark 2.

For this you'll need a flameproof 2.5–3-litre casserole and a large frying pan. First of all you heat the dripping till smoking hot and brown the pieces of meat in it quickly, tossing them around – they should be a deep brown, nutty colour. Now take a draining spoon and transfer them to the casserole. Then, lowering the heat a little, start to fry the prepared vegetables. These, too, should be browned and caramelised a bit at the edges (this is very important for the flavour of the stew). As they brown, transfer them to the casserole to join the meat. Add a knob of butter to the juices left in the frying pan, allow it to melt, then stir in the flour and, with the heat reasonably high, keep stirring and let the flour get brown before gradually adding the hot water, still stirring, as you would for white sauce. When you've added all the water, pour this gravy into the casserole over the meat and vegetables, add some seasoning, the bay leaf, Herbes de Provence and Worcestershire sauce, put a tight lid on and transfer it to the oven to cook for 3 hours.

Just before the end of the cooking time, sift the flour into a basin, mix in the suet, parsley and some seasoning, and enough cold water to make a smooth, elastic dough that leaves the bowl clean. Divide the dough and roll it into 12 small balls. Now transfer the casserole to the top of the stove, on a gentle heat to keep it just simmering, then pop the dumplings in (don't push them into the liquid, just sit them on top). Put the lid back on and let the stew simmer for 25 minutes. Then serve immediately – one snag with dumplings is that they don't like hanging around.

porc au chou

Try to get lean belly of pork cut from the thick end; alternatively, you could use cubed spare rib chops.

570g belly of pork, cubed
110g streaky bacon, rinded and cut into small cubes
2 tablespoons oil
1 large onion, peeled and chopped
1 clove garlic, crushed
10 juniper berries, crushed
275ml dry cider
450g white cabbage, shredded
Chopped parsley
Seasoning

Preheat the oven to 170°C/325°F/gas mark 3.

Heat the oil in a flameproof casserole and soften the onion and garlic in it for about 5 minutes. Then add the cubes of pork and bacon and, with the heat fairly high, brown them to a golden colour, tossing them frequently around. Now lower the heat, add the shredded cabbage and stir to get it all nicely coated with oil; then add the crushed juniper berries followed by the cider. Season, then put a tight-fitting lid on the casserole and cook in the oven for about 1–1¼ hours.

Although this tastes very good, its appearance is deceptive and needs a sprinkling of chopped parsley to jazz it up a bit.

steak and onions in guinness

Serves 2

If you long for a thick, juicy grilled steak and can't afford it, try this recipe with braising steak – it's every bit as good.

350–450g lean braising steak (in two pieces)
2 large onions, peeled and cut into rings
150ml Guinness
Beef dripping
Seasoning

Preheat the oven to 150°C/300°F/gas mark 2.

In a frying pan melt a little dripping and fry the onion rings over a medium heat until they're nicely tinged with brown and starting to caramelise all round the edges. Now remove them to a plate, add a little more dripping to the pan if you need to and brown the meat over a fairly high heat. This browning (on both sides) will help the flavour. Next take a shallow gratin dish or casserole, arrange a layer of onion in it, place the steak on top and season well. Add another layer of onion, pour in the Guinness, cover closely with either a lid or a double sheet of foil and cook near the top of the oven for 2½–3 hours, or until the steak is tender. This goes very well with some creamed potatoes – and with the oven on for that long, you might contemplate cooking another casserole at the same time.

devilled pork slices

For this ask the butcher for 6 lean slices of pork cut from the thick end of the belly.

6 lean slices belly of pork (about 570g)
Seasoning

For the sauce:
1 tablespoon tomato purée
1 tablespoon water
1 tablespoon Worcestershire sauce
1 tablespoon wine vinegar
1 teaspoon clear honey
1 teaspoon made mustard
1 clove garlic, crushed
1 dessertspoon ground ginger

Preheat the oven to 200°C/400°F/gas mark 6.

Trim the rind and any excess fat from the pork, arrange the slices in a single layer in a roasting tin and season them a little. Then thoroughly combine all the sauce ingredients together in a basin and pour this mixture over the pork. Cover the tin with foil and bake in the oven for about 40 minutes. After that, remove the foil and bake for a further 20 minutes or so. Now arrange the pork slices on a warmed serving dish. Keep them warm while you spoon off any fat from the roasting tin, then add about 4 tablespoons of hot water (potato water would be ideal) and stir over a medium heat, scraping the sides and base of the tin. When it reaches simmering point, pour the gravy over the pork and serve with creamy mashed potato.

ground beef curry

This is a good way to 'uplift' 450g of mince, but it *has* to be good-quality mince from a reliable supplier.

450g good-quality minced beef

2 tablespoons groundnut oil

350g onions, peeled and sliced

1 small apple, finely chopped

1 dessertspoon Madras curry powder (or more or less, depending on how hot you like it)

1/2 teaspoon ground ginger

1/2 teaspoon turmeric

Seasoning

2 cloves garlic, crushed

150ml natural yoghurt

150ml hot water mixed with 1 heaped teaspoon tomato purée

Preheat the oven to 150°C/300°F/gas mark 2.

First of all, in a flameproof casserole, heat the oil and soften the sliced onions in it for about 10 minutes. Then turn up the heat, stir in the minced beef and move it around until it's all nicely browned and separate – a wooden fork is good for this. Now turn the heat down and stir in the apple and spices, garlic and some seasoning, followed by the yoghurt and the tomato-and-water mixture. Stir thoroughly, put a lid on and cook in the oven for 2 hours. Serve with rice and mango chutney.

NOTE: *This could be cooked on top of the stove if watched carefully.*

fidget pie

Serves 6

There are many versions of this famous English dish. I don't claim that this recipe
is the authentic one, but it's very good.

700g boned gammon forehock
350g onions, peeled, halved and very thinly sliced
350g cooking apples, peeled, cored and sliced
450g potatoes, peeled and very thinly sliced
275ml dry cider or hot water
Freshly milled black pepper (but no salt)

For the pastry:
225g plain flour
110g lard
A pinch of salt
Water to mix
Milk to glaze

Preheat the oven to 190°C/375°F/gas mark 5.

First remove the rind and excess fat from the gammon, and cut the meat into
quite small pieces. Then gather together all the rest of the ingredients for the pie,
take a 2-litre pie dish and layer the ingredients in this order: first the gammon,
then the onions and apples and finally the potatoes – about 3 layers of each,
finishing off with a layer of potatoes. As you go, sprinkle a little freshly milled
pepper in between the layers. Now pour in the cider. Next prepare the pastry as
described on page 230 (if using ready-made pastry, the equivalent is 335g) and roll
it out. Line the rim of the pie dish with pastry strips and dampen them before
covering with a pastry lid. Now pinch the edges to seal, and decorate the top of
the pie (any pastry left over can be re-rolled and cut into pastry 'leaves'). Lastly,
brush the pastry with milk, make a steam hole in the centre of the pie and sit
the pie dish on a baking sheet. After 30 minutes reduce the heat to 170°C /325°F/
gas mark 3 and cook for a further hour.

bacon with dumplings and parsley sauce

Serves 4

This is both filling and comforting on a really cold day.

A piece of bacon collar weighing about 700g
1 bay leaf
A few parsley stalks
4 smallish onions, peeled and left whole
2 large carrots, scraped and cut in half

For the dumplings:
75g self-raising flour
40g shredded suet
Seasoning

For the sauce:
25g butter
25g plain flour
150ml semi-skimmed milk
275ml stock (use the bacon water)
2 heaped tablespoons chopped parsley

Place the bacon in a good large casserole (it must be large enough to take all the other things). Then cover with cold water, bring to the boil and throw out the water. This will take care of any saltiness. Now pour on some fresh boiling water to just cover the bacon, add the bay leaf and a few parsley stalks, put a lid on and simmer gently for 30 minutes. Then add the peeled whole onions and halved carrots, replace the lid and continue simmering for a further 20 minutes. Meanwhile make the dumplings by mixing the flour, suet and some seasoning with enough cold water to make a smooth, elastic dough, then roll it into 8 small dumplings. When the 20 minutes' cooking time is up, ladle out 275ml of the bacon stock into a measuring jug. Keeping the rest simmering, pop the dumplings in around the bacon – don't push them down, let them float – cover and cook for a further 25 minutes. To make the parsley sauce, melt the butter, stir in the flour and allow to cook for a couple of minutes before adding the milk, reserved bacon stock (plus a little extra if you need it) and the chopped parsley. Serve the bacon cut in slices with the onions, dumplings and carrots, and the sauce in a jug.

navarin of lamb

Serves 4

This is an excellent way of serving middle neck of lamb. I like it best made in the summer with new potatoes, but it can be made in the winter using chunks of old potatoes instead.

900g middle neck of lamb, cut into pieces
Dripping
2 tablespoons plain flour
725ml hot water
1 tablespoon tomato purée
1 clove garlic, crushed
½ teaspoon dried thyme (or a sprig of fresh)
8 small onions, peeled and left whole
6 baby turnips, peeled and quartered
6 small carrots, scraped and cut into 2.5cm lengths
12 very small new potatoes, scraped
1 teaspoon brown sugar
Seasoning

Begin by heating some dripping in a large flameproof casserole. Trim any excess fat from the meat, then season the pieces and fry them in the hot fat until brown on all sides. Now sprinkle in the flour and, keeping the heat fairly low, stir it around to soak up the juices. Next add the hot water, tomato purée, crushed garlic and thyme. Then bring everything gently up to simmering point, giving it a stir now and then. Put the lid on and cook very gently for 45 minutes. While that's happening, using a little more dripping, fry the prepared onions, turnips and carrots. When the 45 minutes are up, add these vegetables to the casserole, along with the scraped potatoes, and bring to simmering point again. Add the sugar, cover and continue to simmer gently for a further 45 minutes.

pork chops
boulangère

For this you can also use spare rib chops or belly of pork strips.

4 pork chops (see above)
1 tablespoon seasoned plain flour
10g butter, plus a little extra
1 tablespoon oil
4 large potatoes, peeled and thinly sliced
1 large onion, peeled and finely chopped
3/4 teaspoon dried sage
275ml stock (or water)
150ml milk
Seasoning

Preheat the oven to 180°C/350°F/gas mark 4.

Dust the chops in seasoned flour, heat the 10g of butter and the oil in a large frying pan and fry the chops on both sides until nicely browned. Then remove the pan from the heat. Now butter a small roasting tin and put a layer of half the potatoes and onion over the base, seasoning them. Lay the browned chops on top and sprinkle them with sage and more seasoning. Cover them with the rest of the onion and then with a final layer of sliced potatoes. Next pour over the mixed stock and milk, add a few flecks of extra butter, cover with greased foil and bake in the oven for about an hour. Then take off the foil, raise the heat to 190°C/375°F/gas mark 5 and bake for a further 30–45 minutes, or until the potatoes are browned on top. This is delicious served with spiced red cabbage.

boiled bacon and pease pudding

Serves 6

Try to get green split peas for this, but yellow will do if you can't buy the green.

A 1.2kg piece boned rolled bacon forehock
1 onion, peeled, halved and each half stuck with 2 cloves
1 large carrot, scraped and cut in chunks
1 bay leaf
A few parsley stalks
450g green split peas
50g butter
1/4–1/2 teaspoon caster sugar
Seasoning

Start off by placing the bacon in a large deep pot and covering it with cold water; then bring it to the boil and as soon as the water reaches boiling point, throw it out and start again with a new lot of cold water. Then add the onion, carrot, bay leaf and parsley stalks. Now wash the peas in a sieve and put them in a large section of linen cloth or double gauze (about 45cm square). Tie it very tightly, but leave the peas plenty of room to expand during the cooking, then pop the bundle of peas into the pot to cook alongside the bacon. Now put a lid on, bring to simmering point, then turn the heat down and simmer gently for about 1¼ hours. After that, have ready a bowl (warmed) containing the butter. Switch off the heat under the pot, remove the bundle of peas, untie it and scrape the peas into the warmed bowl. Now mash them to a purée. Taste and add the sugar and seasoning. If you think the mixture is still on the dry side, add a spoonful of the cooking liquor to moisten it while you skin and carve the bacon. Serve the bacon with the pease pudding on the table for everyone to help themselves – and some parsley sauce would make it extra specially good.

traditional cornish pasties

The quantities given here will make 4 large pasties for 4 people; alternatively, smaller ones could be made for taking on a journey or picnic.

450g chuck steak
1 medium potato, peeled and cut into very thin slices
1 large onion, peeled and chopped very small
1 medium turnip, peeled and cut into very thin slices
1/2 teaspoon Herbes de Provence
450g shortcrust pastry (made with 275g plain flour, 150g lard, a pinch each of salt and pepper, cold water to mix)
1 large egg, beaten
Seasoning

Preheat the oven to 200°C/400°F/gas mark 6.

Cut the steak up into very small thin strips and mix it with the potato, onion, turnip and Herbes de Provence. Season well. Then make the pastry (see page 230; if using ready-made pastry, the equivalent is 425g), divide it into 4 and roll each piece out on a lightly floured surface to a round approximately 20cm in diameter. Place a quarter of the meat mixture in the centre of each round of pastry, then dampen the edges with beaten egg, pull them up to meet in the centre and seal them very thoroughly. Knock up the edges and flute them, then brush the pasties all over with beaten egg, make two small steam holes in each one and place all 4 of them on a lightly greased baking sheet and bake in the oven for 15 minutes. Then reduce the heat to 190°C/375°F/gas mark 5 and continue cooking them for 25 minutes.

steak and kidney hotpot

Serves 6

If you love the delicious combination of steak and kidney but aren't too keen on suet pastry, then this recipe is for you, because instead of pastry it has thickly sliced potatoes on top.

700g chuck steak, trimmed and cut into bite-sized cubes
225g ox kidney, trimmed and cut fairly small
Beef dripping
2 medium onions, peeled and roughly chopped
1 rounded tablespoon plain flour
3/4 teaspoon Worcestershire sauce
275ml beef stock
900g potatoes, peeled and cut into thick slices
Melted butter
Seasoning

Preheat the oven to 150°C/300°F/gas mark 2.

First melt some beef dripping in a large, wide-based saucepan and fry the onions in it to soften for about 5 minutes or so; then turn the heat right up, add the cubes of beef and kidney and cook them to a nutty brown colour – keep stirring and turning the meat as it browns. Now lower the heat a bit, sprinkle in the flour and stir it around to soak up the meat juices. Season well, add the Worcestershire sauce, then gradually stir in the stock and bring to simmering point. Next pour the meat mixture into a casserole or pie dish and arrange the thickly sliced potatoes in layers all over the meat. Season the potatoes, brush them with melted butter, then cover the casserole with a lid or foil and bake in the oven for 2½–3 hours. Before serving remove the lid and brown the potatoes under a very hot grill to get them really crisp.

beef and tomato stew

This is a good recipe for using up overripe tomatoes that are too soft for a salad.

900g chuck steak
3 tablespoons oil
2 onions, peeled and chopped
1 fat clove garlic, crushed
450g tomatoes, skinned (see page 150) and thickly sliced
1 heaped teaspoon Herbes de Provence
1/2 teaspoon brown sugar
Seasoning

Preheat the oven to 150°C/300°F/gas mark 2.

First trim the meat, then cut it into 2.5–4cm cubes. Heat the oil in a flameproof casserole and fry the meat over a fairly high heat until the cubes are nicely browned. Now add the chopped onions and garlic to the pan, turn the heat down a bit and continue to cook for a further 10 minutes, or until the onions are softened. Next add the tomatoes to the casserole with the Herbes de Provence and some seasoning. Stir well, cover the casserole and transfer to the oven to cook slowly for about 2–2½ hours, or until the meat is tender. Then taste and sprinkle in the sugar, and additional seasoning if necessary. This is delicious served with buttered noodles (see page 169).

baked stuffed cabbage leaves

Serves 4–5

This is an anglicised version of the Greek dolmades – stuffed vine leaves.

A 900g–1.35kg head of green cabbage
1 tablespoon oil
1 tablespoon butter
1 onion, peeled and finely chopped
1 clove garlic, crushed
450g lean minced chuck steak
50ml rice, cooked (that's 50ml raw weight)
1 tablespoon chopped parsley
½ teaspoon ground cinnamon
½ teaspoon Herbes de Provence
1 tablespoon tomato purée
1 x 400g tin Italian tomatoes
Seasoning

Preheat the oven to 170°C/325°F/gas mark 3.

First bring a large saucepan of salted water to the boil and place the cabbage in the water, stalk end up. Next bring the water back to the boil and simmer for about 8 minutes; then remove the cabbage and leave it to cool. Working with the cabbage still stalk end up, take a sharp knife and cut the large outer leaves from the main stalk and peel them off one by one. Drain the leaves on kitchen paper – you'll need 15 or 16 leaves altogether. The centre can be used for something else. Now heat the oil and butter together and fry the chopped onion with the garlic gently until the onion is soft and golden. Then add the minced beef and brown it, turning the heat up a bit. Then mix in the rice, parsley, cinnamon, Herbes de Provence and tomato purée, seasoning well. Remove the pan and let the mixture cool. Now make a V-shaped cut to remove the thickest part of the stalk from the base of each leaf, place about a tablespoon of stuffing in the centre of each leaf, fold in the sides and roll the leaf up tightly. Then pack the rolled leaves closely together in a casserole and pour the tomatoes over; cover and cook in the oven for 1½–2 hours.

offal –
but I like you!

Really 'like' isn't quite the word. Offal is either loved or hated (how many lukewarm offal eaters do you know?). But I must be careful here: often it's indelicate promotion that is to blame. We're all seen those ghastly Technicolor pictures in magazines that thrust the whole lot at us in its raw state. Ugh!

The word itself is scarcely a euphemism (Margaret Costa in her delightful *Four Seasons Cookbook* called it, pointedly, 'Awful Offal'). I frequently call it 'Spare Parts', because that's what it is – lots of nutritious bits and pieces full of potential and flavour. In Britain we've never really made the most of it because we've always had so much meat anyway. But now the time has come to learn from our French cousins, who have always had to make every bit of precious meat go as far as possible.

Fear not, I'm not about to offer you a Pig's Tail Ragout or some baked stuffed intestines. Instead I'm sticking to the more familiar and available liver and kidneys, etc., which, although they are expensive, seem to go much further (so you need much less to make a meal). Once again, though, I do stress the seasons. English lamb's liver and kidney will be plentiful from June to October. Oxtails, ox kidney and liver will all be at their cheapest in the winter from about October. Pork offal, however, seems to be plentiful all the year round.

braised stuffed hearts

6 lambs' hearts
Seasoned plain flour
1 tablespoon butter
1 tablespoon oil
1 large onion, peeled and chopped
150ml stock or water
150ml dry cider
2 teaspoons each butter and flour, worked to a paste
1 teaspoon redcurrant jelly

For the stuffing:

3 tablespoons butter
1 small onion, peeled and finely chopped
50g fresh white breadcrumbs
1 small cooking apple, peeled and chopped
Rind and juice of 1 orange
$\frac{1}{2}$ teaspoon Herbes de Provence
3 tablespoons chopped parsley
Seasoning

Preheat the oven to 180°C/350°F/gas mark 4.

First wash the hearts thoroughly. With a pair of scissors cut out all the tubes and the dividing wall in the centre of each heart to make a neat pocket for the stuffing. Prepare the stuffing by heating the butter in a small saucepan and gently frying the onion until softened. Mix the onion and any fat in the pan with the remaining stuffing ingredients. Now stuff the cavities in the hearts and secure them at the top with small skewers. Roll the hearts in seasoned flour, then brown in a casserole in the remaining butter and the oil. Stir in the chopped onion, cook over a gentle heat until softened, then add the stock and cider. Bring to simmering point, cover and cook in the oven for about 2½–3 hours, or until the hearts are tender. Drain and arrange them in a warmed serving dish. Bring the remaining pan juices to the boil and add small pieces of the butter and flour paste, stirring quickly. Then add the redcurrant jelly, taste and season. Pour the sauce over the hearts and serve.

pork kidneys with mustard cream sauce

Serves 4

Pork kidneys soaked overnight have a much milder flavour and, as they're fairly reasonably priced, it's worth going to the trouble.

4 pork kidneys, soaked overnight in cold water
50g lard
1 large onion, peeled and chopped
1 clove garlic, crushed
1 teaspoon plain flour
150ml stock or hot water
150ml dry cider
A generous pinch of thyme
1½ teaspoons mustard powder
1½ teaspoons Dijon mustard
2 tablespoons double cream or half-fat crème fraîche
A pinch of cayenne pepper
Seasoning

First put the kettle on to boil. Then, after draining the kidneys, slice them across into 5mm-thick medallion-shaped slices and snip out the white cores using a pair of scissors. Now transfer them to a sieve and rinse them with a kettleful of boiling water; leave them to drain thoroughly and dry them in some kitchen paper. Next, in a cooking pot, melt the lard and soften the onion and garlic in it for 5 minutes. Then turn the heat up to high, add the drained and dried kidneys and brown them on all sides. Next lower the heat and stir in the flour to soak up the juices before adding the stock, cider, thyme and seasoning. Now put a lid on and simmer gently for 45 minutes. Meanwhile mix the mustards with the cream, add a pinch of cayenne pepper, then stir this into the cooked kidneys. Cook for a minute or two, then serve with buttered noodles (see page 169) or rice.

spiced kidneys
in yoghurt

The imported frozen lambs' kidneys we get in the winter are never quite good enough to be served 'straight' but are perfectly fine in a curry like this.

6 lambs' kidneys, skinned
2 tablespoons groundnut oil
2 medium-sized onions, peeled and thinly sliced
1 clove garlic, crushed
1 tablespoon tomato purée
2 teaspoons ground coriander
1 teaspoon turmeric
¼ cumin seeds
150ml natural yoghurt
150ml stock
Salt
¼ teaspoon chilli powder (or according to how hot you like it)

To prepare the kidneys, halve them lengthways and snip out the cores using a sharp pair of kitchen scissors. Now heat the oil in a saucepan and fry the kidneys over a fairly high heat until lightly browned; then transfer them to a plate using a draining spoon. Next fry the sliced onions and garlic in the juices remaining in the pan until the onions are softened and golden. Then stir in the tomato purée, spices and yoghurt, and add the stock. Bring the sauce to simmering point and continue to simmer very gently for about 15 minutes. Now taste it and flavour the sauce with salt and as much chilli powder as you want – but be careful, it is lethal if you add too much. Then return the kidneys (and any juices) to the pan, cover and simmer gently for 20 minutes. Taste again and season if it needs it. This is nice served with buttered noodles (see page 169) and an extra dollop of yoghurt if available.

kidney stroganoff

Serves 4

I think a Stroganoff made with lambs' kidneys is even nicer than one made with fillet steak.

12 lambs' kidneys, skinned
1 medium onion
60g butter
225g mushrooms
150ml soured cream
Seasoning
Freshly grated nutmeg

Begin by peeling the onion and slicing it into very thin rings. Now slice the rings in half and separate them to give you moon-shaped slivers. Melt 50g of the butter in a large frying pan and gently soften the onion in it for 10 minutes. Meanwhile wipe the mushrooms, slice the stalks and caps thinly, then add them to the onion, stirring them around, and cook for a further 5 minutes. The kidneys should be first halved lengthways and the cores snipped out, then cut into the thinnest slices possible. Turn the heat up a bit under the pan, add the kidney slices and brown them quickly, constantly turning the pieces over. Now turn the heat right down and stir in the soured cream, adding seasoning and nutmeg, and let everything simmer very gently for 5 minutes. Just before serving, stir in the remaining butter, then serve immediately with plain boiled rice.

liver and bacon kebabs with stuffing

Serves 4

I like to serve these with brown rice and a home-made tomato sauce.

350g lambs' liver
About 6 rashers streaky bacon, rinded and cut into small squares
40g dripping or butter, melted

For the stuffing:
110g fresh white breadcrumbs
50g butter, melted
1 teaspoon grated onion
1/2 teaspoon Herbes de Provence
A pinch of powdered mace
1 large egg
Seasoning
About 2 tablespoons semi-skimmed milk (to bind)

First cut the lambs' liver into bite-sized pieces, roughly all the same size. Then, to make the stuffing, simply combine all the stuffing ingredients together in a bowl and mix thoroughly, with enough milk to bind. Next form the mixture into about 12 balls. Pierce one of them on to a flattened skewer, then thread the meats on (liver, bacon, liver, bacon, then another ball of stuffing and so on), filling 4 skewers. Now brush the kebabs liberally with melted dripping or butter and cook them under a fairly hot grill for about 10 minutes, turning and basting evenly at regular intervals. Serve hot, straight from the grill to the table.

kidneys with chipolatas

A cheaper version, this one, of the famous Kidneys Turbigo.

6 lambs' kidneys, skinned
2 tablespoons butter
2 tablespoons oil
3 slices bread, taken from a large white loaf
6 pork chipolata sausages
1 medium onion, peeled and chopped
275ml stock
1 teaspoon cornflour
1 teaspoon mustard powder
1 teaspoon wine vinegar
½ teaspoon brown sugar
2 pinches of cayenne pepper
Seasoning

First put a serving dish in a warm oven, then heat the butter and oil in a frying pan. Cut the bread into triangles and fry on both sides until crisp and golden. Drain the bread well on kitchen paper and keep hot in the oven. Next fry the chipolatas and keep these warm too. Halve the kidneys lengthways and snip out the cores, then cook them for about 3–4 minutes. Arrange them with the chipolatas on the serving dish. Now fry the onion gently until soft and golden and, using a draining spoon, arrange it over the kidneys and sausages. Next add the stock to the pan and boil briskly, scraping the base and sides of the pan, until the stock is reduced by half. Now blend the cornflour, mustard and vinegar in a small basin, stir into the stock, bring to the boil and simmer for 2 or 3 minutes. Sprinkle in the sugar and a couple of pinches of cayenne, season to taste, then pour the sauce over the kidneys and sausages, and serve with the bread triangles.

liver and vegetable hotpot

Serves 4

450g of ox liver will be plenty for 4 people if you add some bacon and vegetables and a thick crusty potato topping.

450g ox liver
1 tablespoon seasoned plain flour
1 carrot, scraped and cut into chunks
1 stick celery, cut into chunks
50g swedes, peeled and cut into small chunks
110g streaky bacon rashers, rinded
3 largish onions, peeled and sliced
1 teaspoon dried sage
Approx. 570ml stock or water
1 teaspoon Worcestershire sauce
900g potatoes, peeled and cut into thick slices
A little beef dripping, melted
Seasoning

Preheat the oven to 170°C/325°F/gas mark 3.

Cut the liver into slices about 5mm thick, then toss the slices in the seasoned flour. Now in a casserole arrange the slices of liver, cut vegetables, bacon and onions, adding seasoning and a little dried sage. When everything is in, add enough stock or water to barely cover the liver etc., add the Worcestershire sauce and cover everything with a thick layer of potatoes overlapping each other. Now add a final sprinkle of seasoning, cover closely and place the casserole in the oven for about 1½ hours. Then take the lid off, brush the potatoes with a little melted beef dripping and increase the heat to 200°C/400°F/gas mark 6 to let them get brown and crusty on top – this will take about another 30 minutes.

liver with crisp-fried onions

Nothing is nicer with liver than some crispy deep-fried onions – and for this recipe, buy the liver from a helpful butcher who'll slice it very thinly for you.

450g lambs' liver
Groundnut oil for deep-frying
50g butter
2 tablespoons oil
Seasoned plain flour
2 medium onions, peeled and sliced in thin rings
Plain flour
1 large egg white
275ml beef stock (or potato water)
Seasoning

The best way to do this is to heat the groundnut oil in a deep-fryer (to 180°C/350°F) and melt the butter and oil for the liver in a frying pan simultaneously, so that you can cook both the liver and the onions at more or less the same time. Also have some serving dishes keeping warm in the oven with some kitchen paper on them to absorb any excess oil. The liver slices should be coated in seasoned flour and fried quickly over a high heat in the butter and oil (about 1 minute on each side), then kept warm. The onions should be separated into thin rings, dipped first in plain flour, then in stiffly beaten egg white, and deep-fried till golden and crisp (for 1 or 2 minutes – it's best to do them a few at a time). Finally sprinkle 1 level tablespoon of plain flour into the pan juices left from the liver and cook it for a minute or two, then gradually stir in the stock to make a gravy, seasoning well. Serve the liver garnished with the onions, and the gravy separately.

kidney-stuffed onions

These are very good served with a mild-flavoured cheese sauce and some savoury rice.

4 large Spanish onions
6 lambs' kidneys, skinned
50g butter, plus a little extra
2 teaspoons plain flour
4 tablespoons stock
A few drops of Worcestershire sauce
1/4 teaspoon Herbes de Provence
Seasoning

Peel the onions first, then parboil them in a covered pan with about 2.5cm of water in it – give them about 40–45 minutes to half cook. Then drain them and leave them on one side till they are cool enough to handle. Now preheat the oven to 190°C/375°F/gas mark 5, carefully remove the centres from the onions (keep them for soups or stews, etc.) and place the onions in a well-buttered gratin dish. Next halve the lambs' kidneys lengthways and snip out the cores, then chop them into fairly small pieces and fry them in 50g of butter for about 5 minutes. Now stir in the flour, cook for a further minute or two and then gradually stir in the stock, a couple of drops of Worcestershire sauce and the Herbes de Provence. Season well, simmer for a minute or two, then spoon the mixture into the hollowed onions. Add a small knob of butter to each onion and bake in the oven for 30–35 minutes, basting with the juices from time to time.

oxtail hotpot

1 oxtail, cut into joints
50–75g beef dripping, plus a little extra (melted)
½ teaspoon Herbes de Provence
1 small turnip, peeled and cut into chunks
1 small swede, peeled and cut into chunks
2 medium carrots, scraped and cut into chunks
2 sticks celery, cut into chunks
3 small onions, peeled and left whole
1 bay leaf
1 heaped tablespoon plain flour
570ml hot water
2 teaspoons Worcestershire sauce
450g potatoes, peeled and cut into thick slices
Seasoning

Preheat the oven to 150°C/300°F/gas mark 2.

In the largest frying pan you have, get the dripping really hot and quickly brown the pieces of oxtail to a deep brown colour. Then transfer them with a draining spoon to a large casserole, season them and sprinkle with Herbes de Provence. Follow the oxtail with the vegetables (except the potatoes), browning these too just a little, and arrange them all around and over the pieces of oxtail. Add a little more seasoning and the bay leaf. Now stir the flour into the juices left in the frying pan and allow it to brown before gradually adding the hot water, followed by the Worcestershire sauce. Then transfer the liquid to the casserole (sieving it if it's gone lumpy) and finally arrange the thickly sliced potatoes over the top. Put a lid on and bake for 3 hours, taking the lid off 30 minutes before the end, and finally brushing the potatoes with a little melted dripping and browning them until crisp under a hot grill for a few minutes before serving. This dish doesn't really need any extra vegetables to go with it.

kidneys in gravy

A very quick little casserole for 2 people that can be made in about 30 minutes from start to finish.

6 lambs' kidneys, skinned
50g dripping or melted kidney fat
1 large onion, peeled and chopped
4 rashers unsmoked streaky bacon, rinded and chopped
110g dark flat mushrooms
1 dessertspoon plain flour
1 heaped teaspoon tomato purée
1 teaspoon Worcestershire sauce
275ml hot water (or potato water)
Seasoning

Melt the fat in a large saucepan and soften the onion in it for 5 minutes. Next add the chopped bacon, cooking for another 5 minutes, then add the mushrooms and stir them around for a minute or two. Cut the kidneys into halves, lengthways and snip out the core with a pair of scissors. Now turn the heat up under the saucepan, add the kidneys and brown them lightly, stirring them around a bit. Next sprinkle in the flour and stir to soak up the juices. Now stir the tomato purée and Worcestershire sauce into the hot water, then gradually add it to the pan, stirring as you do so. Season, then put a lid on and simmer very gently for about 20 minutes. Serve with some creamy mashed potato.

oxtail braised in cider

Alas, oxtail gets more expensive, but it's very plentiful in the autumn and just needs some vegetables to eke it out.

1.1–1.35kg oxtail, cut into joints
Beef dripping
110g streaky bacon, rinded and cut into cubes
3 large carrots, scraped and cut in thick chunks
2 large onions, peeled and sliced
25g plain flour
425ml hot beef stock
425ml dry cider
1/2 teaspoon Herbes de Provence
1 teaspoon juniper berries, crushed
1 clove garlic, crushed
1 bay leaf
Seasoning
Chopped parsley

Preheat the oven to 150°C/300°F/gas mark 2.

Start by melting the dripping in a large flameproof casserole, get it really hot, then brown the pieces of oxtail, 2 or 3 at a time. Remove them to a plate as they brown, then brown the bacon and chunks of carrot, and remove them to a plate as well. Next fry the onions till browned at the edges. Turn the heat down a bit, then stir in the flour to soak up the juices before gradually adding the stock and cider. Now return the meat, bacon and carrots to the casserole, add the Herbes de Provence, juniper, garlic and bay leaf, and season. Put a close-fitting lid on, transfer to the oven and cook for 3 hours. Just before serving, skim off any fat from the surface and sprinkle with chopped parsley.

liver casserole

This is a recipe for summer, when English lambs' liver is plentiful.

570g lambs' liver, cut into 5mm-thick slices
Seasoned plain flour
25g butter
1 tablespoon oil
2 medium onions, peeled and thinly sliced
225g new carrots, washed and cut into 2.5cm lengths
900g small new potatoes, scraped
450g tomatoes, skinned (see page 150) and sliced
275ml stock
$1/2$ teaspoon Herbes de Provence
1 tablespoon tomato purée
Seasoning

Preheat the oven to 180°C/350°F/gas mark 4.

Begin by drying the liver slices with some kitchen paper, then lightly coat the pieces in well-seasoned flour. Next heat the butter and oil together in a large frying pan and soften the sliced onions in it over a low heat for about 10 minutes. Now arrange half the floured liver slices in the base of a deep ovenproof casserole and cover with a layer of onions, carrots and scraped new potatoes, followed by half the sliced tomatoes. Then repeat all over again, finishing up with a layer of tomatoes. Combine the stock, Herbes de Provence and tomato purée together in a jug, season, pour this into the casserole, cover closely and bake for approximately 1½ hours, or until the vegetables are tender.

liver and onion yorkshire pud

If you think 225g lambs' liver might not be enough for 4 people, try this!

225g lambs' liver
1 large onion, peeled and chopped
Lard

For the batter:

110g plain flour
1 large egg
150ml milk mixed with 150ml water
¼ teaspoon chopped thyme (fresh or dried)
Seasoning

Preheat the oven to 220°C/425°/F/gas mark 7.

Place a thick-based meat roasting tin (measuring approximately 23 x 16cm at the base) on a high shelf in the oven with about 25g of lard in it. While it's heating through, prepare the batter by sifting the flour into a bowl, making a well in the centre of the flour, dropping the egg in and whisking it gradually, incorporating the flour and adding the milk-and-water mixture by degrees until you have a smooth batter. Add seasoning and the thyme. Now cut the liver into thinnish strips about 2.5cm in length. Fry the onion in a little more lard to soften (about 10 minutes), then add the liver and, with the heat fairly high, move it about and turn it so that it browns nicely – this should take around 2–3 minutes (be careful not to overcook it). Now take the tin out of the oven, place it over a low heat on top of the stove to keep it sizzling, then spoon in the liver and onions and their juices, and pour the batter over. Return it to the oven and cook for about 35–40 minutes.

faggots and peas

A real old-fashioned favourite, this one, full of flavour and not too expensive.
Caul fat looks like lacy curtains and you can get it from a good butcher if you
order it in advance.

450g pig's liver, cut into 2.5cm cubes
110g unsmoked bacon, cut into 2.5cm cubes
175g pork back fat, cut into 2.5cm cubes
2 medium onions, peeled
420ml stock
50g fresh white breadcrumbs
1 teaspoon Herbes de Provence
$^{1}/_{4}$ teaspoon powdered mace
A piece of caul fat, about 90cm square
Seasoning

Then

725ml chicken stock
1 onion, peeled and quartered
450g green split peas
50g butter

Preheat the oven to 180°C/350°F/gas mark 4.

First place the liver, bacon, back fat and onions in a casserole and pour in the
stock. Bake this for 45 minutes, then pour the contents of the casserole into a
large sieve set over a bowl. Now mince the cooked meats through the fine blade
of the mincer, and mix them with the breadcrumbs, herbs and spice. Then
season well and form the mixture into 8 little cake shapes. Next rinse the caul
fat in a bowl of warm water, drain well and spread it out carefully. Cut out 8 x
15cm squares, wrap the faggots in them and pack together in a greased baking
dish just big enough to hold them. Now skim the fat from the stock and pour
275ml of the stock over the faggots in the baking dish and bake (uncovered) for
about 45 minutes.

To cook the peas, put the chicken stock and quartered onion into a pan and bring to the boil. Add the split peas to the pan and bring back to the boil, turn down the heat, then cover and simmer very gently for 1½ hours or until the peas are tender. Then mash with the butter and add seasoning to taste (if the mixture is a little dry, add some of the remaining stock from the faggot recipe). Serve the peas with the faggots and the juices poured over.

Alas, there's almost no whole bacon around that can be cut into cubes, but packets of lardons (ready-cut cubes) are widely available.

bangers
are beautiful

Almost every country in the world has some sort of national sausage.

I've seen them threaded on skewers over glowing charcoal on the streets of Istanbul and simmering in garlic-laced bean pots in the Tuscan hills, while in France there are dozens of varieties, from the spicy coarse-cut saucissons of Provence to the pale, gutsy andouillettes of the Lyonnais.

In Britain we have bangers. They burst and spread themselves out over the pan, amalgamating with each other before charring, crisp and black outside and pink and soft within. Well, they say it takes all sorts, but my complaint is that we really don't have enough sorts: the bran-filled monster I've just described gets awfully boring. Fortunately, we do have a few 'beautiful' bangers, made by butchers up and down the country who take a pride in their own particular recipe (my own butcher's are excellent). And if you haven't got a butcher who makes good ones, I suggest you try to get hold of some from better supermarkets.

Good sausages, it's true, are more expensive but, because they contain more meat, they don't shrivel and shrink in the cooking, releasing floods of watery fat. Having hunted down the perfect banger, these recipes offered here will help to make them go a bit further (or, if you're prepared to do without skins, you can even make your own).

Yes, bangers are still beautiful and have come on in leaps and bounds since the 70s – certainly there are very few bursting bran-filled ones now. Top of the range can be expensive, but there are still bargains and cut-price versions on offer.

home-made sausages

450g minced pork
50g shredded beef suet
$1/2$ small onion, peeled and grated
2 thick slices bread from a large loaf (crusts off)
$1 1/2$ tablespoons semi-skimmed milk
3 fresh sage leaves, chopped small (or $1/4$ teaspoon dried)
$1/4$ whole nutmeg, grated
$1/4$ teaspoon chopped thyme (fresh or dried)
$1 1/2$ tablespoons seasoned plain flour
Lard
Seasoning

Take a large bowl and mix the meat and suet together very thoroughly, then add the grated onion. Soak the bread in the milk, squeeze the excess liquid out, and pop that in too, then mix very thoroughly. Now add the sage, nutmeg, and thyme and season well. Take care to give it a thorough mixing – it's most important. Next take about a tablespoon of the mixture, press it together, roll it into a sausage shape on a clean surface, then roll it in seasoned flour – and carry on like that until all your sausages are made. To cook, fry them in hot lard to brown all round, then reduce the heat to medium to cook them through. They take about 25 minutes in all. Drain them on crumpled kitchen paper and serve with sauté potatoes and a crisp salad, or with creamy mashed potato, mustard or chutney.

sausages with
chilli sauce

450g pork sausages

1 whole fresh red chilli (or ¼ teaspoon chilli powder)

1 tablespoon olive oil

1 onion, peeled and chopped

1 small green pepper, deseeded and diced

2 cloves garlic, crushed

1 x 400g tin Italian tomatoes

1 teaspoon Herbes de Provence

¼ teaspoon sugar

1 teaspoon tomato purée

Seasoning

Begin by deseeding the chilli (if you are using a whole one), discarding the fiery seeds and chopping the red part finely. Now heat the olive oil in a flameproof casserole or saucepan, brown the sausages all round and, using a draining spoon, remove them from the pan. Next stir the onion, green pepper and garlic into the fat remaining in the pan and cook gently until softened (about 10 minutes). Now stir in the tomatoes, Herbes de Provence, sugar and tomato purée, bring up to simmering point, then return the sausages to the pan. Allow to simmer very gently (uncovered), stirring occasionally, for about 25 minutes until the tomatoes are reduced to a thick sauce-like consistency. Then taste and season before serving. This is very good served with buttered noodles (see page 169) or with creamy mashed potato.

sausage-stuffed onions

If you can, try to get the very largest (preferably Spanish) onions for this.

4 large Spanish onions
225g good sausagemeat
40g butter, plus a little extra
1/2 teaspoon dried sage
1 clove garlic, crushed
50g mushrooms, finely chopped
25g dry white breadcrumbs
1 small cooking apple, peeled, cored and chopped
150ml natural yoghurt
2 tablespoons chopped parsley
Paprika
Seasoning

Preheat the oven to 200°C/400°F/gas mark 6.

After you've peeled the onions, put them in a large pan of boiling salted water. Bring the water back to the boil, cover and simmer gently for about 30 minutes. Then drain the onions and leave them to cool. Now cut a thin cap from the top of each onion and scoop out the centres, leaving a fairly substantial shell. Arrange the onion cases (packing them closely together) in a deep, buttered baking dish. Then chop up the onion you removed. Next heat the 40g of butter in a frying pan and measure 3 tablespoons of the chopped onion into it. Fry briskly for a minute or two before adding the sausagemeat and sage – mashing them down with a fork until the sausagemeat is separate and evenly coloured. Then stir in the garlic, mushrooms, breadcrumbs and apple. Taste and season (some sausagemeats come quite highly seasoned to start with, so do taste it first). Now remove the pan from the heat and stir in a tablespoon of yoghurt together with the parsley. Put the mixture into the onion shells – if it seems a little too much, just pile it up on top. Then transfer the baking dish to the top half of the oven and bake for 20 minutes. Finally put a blob of yoghurt on each onion and dust with paprika. Replace in the oven for a further 5–10 minutes and serve with creamy mashed potato.

NOTE: *Any bits of onion centres left over can be used for soups or stocks.*

toad-in-the-hole
with sage and onions

Not an attractive name, admittedly, but it's a delicious classic, especially if you make it with good-quality pork sausages, a little sage and fried onion rings.

450g pure pork sausages
Beef dripping or lard
2 medium onions, peeled and sliced thinly
175g plain flour
2 large eggs
175ml semi-skimmed milk
110ml water
1 teaspoon dried sage
Seasoning

Preheat the oven to 220°C/425°F/gas mark 7.

First put a tablespoon of dripping into a solid-based roasting tin (base measuring about 23 x 18cm) and pop it into the oven to heat. Then in a frying pan melt some more fat and brown the onions for about 5 minutes or so until they have softened a bit. Remove them to a plate and lightly brown the sausages all round – again for about 5 minutes. While they're browning, make the batter by sifting the flour into a bowl. Make a well in the middle, drop the eggs in and, using an electric hand-whisk (or a fork), whisk the eggs, incorporating the flour and adding the milk and water mixed together first. Season the batter and add the sage. When the fat in the tin starts to sizzle, take it out of the oven and keep it sizzling by placing it on top of the stove over a medium heat. Then put in the sausages with the onions on top of them and, making sure the fat is still very hot, pour in the batter. Quickly shake the tin to get the batter all round the base of the sausages, etc., then transfer the tin back to the highest shelf of the oven and let it bake for about 40 minutes, or until puffy and crisp. Serve straight away, with gravy.

frankfurters with hot potato salad

If you have a delicatessen in your area, try to get the really long frankfurters for this recipe, as they're generally much better than the supermarket variety.

8 large frankfurters
700g potatoes
6 tablespoons oil
1 medium onion, peeled, halved and thinly sliced
1 clove garlic, crushed
2 tablespoons cider vinegar
1 teaspoon made mustard
A few drops of Tabasco sauce
2 tablespoons chopped parsley
Seasoning

To start with, scrub the potatoes well (but don't peel them), then boil them in salted water until they're just tender. While that's happening, heat 2 tablespoons of oil in a separate pan and fry the onion and crushed garlic for 2 or 3 minutes. Then add the remaining oil and the cider vinegar, stir in the mustard, Tabasco and seasoning, and heat until boiling. Then turn the heat low and, at this stage, poach the frankfurters (but check with the supplier for how long, because it does vary). Next drain the boiled potatoes, put them in a warm serving bowl and pour over the hot oil and vinegar mixture. Now sprinkle with the parsley and, using a sharp knife, roughly chop the potatoes. Then serve with the hot cooked frankfurters on top, and have some extra mustard on the table.

NOTE: *I always like to leave the skins on the potatoes, but if you prefer you can peel them off as soon as the potatoes are drained.*

bangers braised in cider

Serves 3

I always use herb-flavoured sausages for this, but any sort of pork sausage will do.

450g pork sausages
Lard
225g lean streaky bacon in one piece, then cut into cubes (or use lardons)
225g small button onions, peeled
1 heaped teaspoon plain flour
275ml dry cider
1 clove garlic, crushed
1 bay leaf
1/2 teaspoon Herbes de Provence
1 Cox's apple, cored and cut into rings (no need to peel it)
A little butter
Seasoning

Preheat the oven to 180°C/350°F/gas mark 4.

Take a large flameproof casserole, melt a little lard in it and brown the sausages all round. Then, using a slotted spoon, remove them to a plate while you brown the bacon cubes and onions lightly. When they're done, sprinkle in the flour to soak up the juices, then gradually stir in the cider. Now pop the sausages back in, plus the garlic, bay leaf and Herbes de Provence and a little seasoning. Put a lid on when it all comes to simmering point and then transfer to the oven for 30 minutes. When the 30 minutes is up, remove the lid and cook for a further 20–30 minutes. Before serving, fry the apple rings in butter until soft and garnish the casserole with them. This is lovely served with spicy red cabbage.

sausages with lentils

700g sausages

175g dried green lentils (not the orange ones)

1 large onion, peeled and chopped

2 cloves garlic, crushed

1 level tablespoon butter

1 tablespoon oil

1 x 400g tin Italian tomatoes

1 level teaspoon sugar

2 or 3 pinches of Herbes de Provence

1 bay leaf

Seasoning

Rinse the lentils, place them in a saucepan with enough water to cover (don't add any salt), bring them to simmering point and cook gently for about 30 minutes, or until they are tender but not disintegrating. Now drain them, keeping the cooking liquid. Then fry the onion and garlic in the butter and oil, add the tomatoes, sugar, Herbes de Provence and bay leaf, and let it all simmer gently (without a lid) until the liquid reduces and it becomes rather thick – you may need to stir it now and then. Now in a frying pan brown the sausages all over in a little more oil. Then, using a draining spoon, transfer them to the tomato mixture. Add the lentils now and approximately 275ml of the liquid they were cooked in. Stir well and continue cooking over a very gentle heat for about 30 minutes – again without a lid. If the mixture begins to look dry add a little more liquid. Taste and add seasoning if necessary before serving.

pork sausages with cider sauce

I first made this using red wine, but now I've switched to cider and it's every bit as good.

450g good-quality pork sausages
25g lard
1 onion, peeled and chopped
4 slices streaky bacon, rinded and chopped
2 teaspoons plain flour
110g dark mushrooms, sliced
110ml dry cider
150ml stock or water
2 teaspoons tomato purée
¼ teaspoon Herbes de Provence
1 teaspoon redcurrant jelly
Seasoning

First gently brown the sausages all over in the lard; then, using a draining spoon, transfer them to a plate and keep them on one side. Now add the onion and the bacon to the fat remaining in the pan and cook these for about 10 minutes, or until the onion is soft. Then sprinkle in the flour and stir it round to soak up the juices. Add the mushrooms and cook for 5 more minutes before stirring in the cider and stock. Next add the tomato purée, Herbes de Provence and redcurrant jelly, bring to simmering point, taste and season. Cook gently without a cover for about 15 minutes. These are delicious served with some creamy mashed potatoes or even some Onion Rice (see page 166).

sausages boulangère

These are nice served with some freshly made sharp English mustard.

450g sausages
Oil
700g potatoes, peeled and very thinly sliced
1 medium onion, peeled and finely chopped
25g butter
150ml semi-skimmed milk
150ml stock or water
1 teaspoon Herbes de Provence
Seasoning

Preheat the oven to 180°C/350°F/gas mark 4.

Brown the sausages all over in a little oil in a frying pan – this should take around 5 or 6 minutes – and while that's happening put a smear of butter round the base of a casserole. Then put in a layer of the potatoes, a sprinkling of onion and seasoning, and repeat the layers until all the potatoes are in, finishing off with a few flecks of butter. Now remove the browned sausages from the pan, using a draining spoon, and place these on top of the potatoes. Sprinkle in the Herbes de Provence, pour in the milk and water, cover the casserole with a piece of foil, place it in the oven and bake for about 45 minutes. Then remove the foil and bake for a further 15–20 minutes, or until the potatoes are tender when tested with a thin skewer.

purée of peas with sausages

This makes a nice accompaniment to 450g of ordinary fried sausages.

450g sausages
450g green split peas
1 small onion, peeled and stuck with 4 cloves
1/4 teaspoon Herbes de Provence
2 tablespoons half-fat crème fraîche
25g butter
Seasoning
Freshly grated nutmeg

Put the split peas in a pan and cover them with cold water. Bring this to the boil very slowly, remove from the heat and leave to soak for 1 hour. Then drain the peas and place them back in the saucepan together with the onion stuck with cloves, the Herbes de Provence and some salt. Cover again with cold water and simmer till tender (about 20 minutes). Then drain the peas again and rub them through a sieve into the top of a double saucepan (or a basin sitting over some simmering water); stir in the crème fraîche and butter, and leave it like this for about 20 minutes, stirring now and then until it becomes very thick. Meanwhile, fry the sausages. Season the peas with freshly milled black pepper and freshly grated nutmeg, together with more salt if they need it. Serve the purée piled on to a plate with the fried sausages on top.

poor man's cassoulet

This is a much cheaper and easier version than the original classic cassoulet. Nevertheless, do try to get decent bangers if possible.

450g pork sausages
350g long haricot beans
Groundnut oil
225g streaky bacon in one piece, then cut into cubes (or use lardons)
3 medium onions, peeled and sliced
3 cloves garlic, finely chopped
1 1/2 tablespoons tomato purée
3/4 teaspoon Herbes de Provence
110g fresh white breadcrumbs
Seasoning

Preheat the oven to 140°C/275°F/gas mark 1.

Either soak the beans overnight or wash them, place them in a saucepan, cover with plenty of cold water, bring to the boil and let them boil for 1 minute. Then turn off the heat and let them soak for 2–3 hours. Then, in a flameproof casserole, heat some oil and brown the sausages to a nice golden colour. Remove them to a plate, then colour the bacon cubes a little and transfer them to join the waiting sausages. Now in the juices left in the pan soften the onions and garlic for 10 minutes, and while that's happening drain the beans (reserving their soaking water). Put a layer of beans into the cooking pot containing the onion and garlic, then add half the sausages and bacon, followed by more beans, the rest of the sausages and bacon, and finally the rest of the beans. Next measure 725ml of the soaking water, stir 1½ tablespoons of tomato purée into it, along with the Herbes de Provence and some seasoning – but be sparing with the salt (because of the bacon). Pour this over the rest of the ingredients, then cover and bake for 2 hours. Then take the lid off, sprinkle the breadcrumbs all over the top, and bake (without a lid) for a further hour. This is very rich and hefty, so a green salad is really all you need to go with it.

cook for
victory

1976 must surely go down as the year Britain took to the spade. Was it the potato crisis, the exorbitant prices or the media jumping on another bandwagon? Where once the bookshelves were dominated by cookery books, there are now an equal number of baffling and bewildering gardening books and step-by-step part-works with titles like *Grow It and Cook It* and *Grow It and Freeze It.*

Very commendable, and I hope the harvest proved worth all the sweat, because for too long (while meat was plentiful) vegetables have played a secondary role, just a little something to help the meat go down. I believe this is changing now, if only because we've travelled abroad more and been made more aware of the full potential of vegetables – that what might have been a simple uninspiring meal can be transformed into something much more special by the clever treatment of vegetables.

Take marrow, one of our cheapest and most easily grown vegetables, yet so often relegated to a watery white sauce. Try it on its own with tomatoes, garlic and crushed coriander seeds, and see what I mean. If you grow fresh herbs, then do make some herb butter (by chopping up a mixture of herbs and combining them with butter) and just swirl a knob of this around cooked new potatoes or carrots or cauliflower – it instantly puts them into the four-star bracket. All the recipes here attempt to make the most of vegetables, whether they're to be eaten on their own or used to jazz up cold meat, sausages or other fairly simple dishes.

What potato crisis? Well, drought in Europe, a virulent blight and panic in the potato futures market in 1976 caused the price of spuds to rise dramatically. Difficult at the time but now thankfully all forgotten.

broad bean salad

Serves 2

700g broad beans (that's 700g before shelling)
1 rasher lean bacon, rinded
1 tablespoon chopped herbs (I use a mixture of tarragon, marjoram and parsley)
4 spring onions, finely chopped
crisp lettuce leaves

For the vinaigrette dressing:
1 teaspoon crushed rock salt
1 dessertspoon lemon juice
1 dessertspoon wine vinegar
½ clove garlic, crushed
1 teaspoon mustard powder
4 dessertspoons oil
Freshly milled black pepper

First cook the bacon until it's really crisp, then drain it well and crumble it into very small pieces. Next make the dressing by dissolving the salt in the lemon juice and vinegar for 30 minutes, then shake it with the rest of the ingredients in a screw-top jar to get everything thoroughly amalgamated. Now cook the shelled beans in a very little salted water for about 5 minutes – it's very important not to overcook them or they'll lose their colour and go mushy – then drain them thoroughly and toss them in the dressing while they're still warm. When they're cool, toss in the herbs, finely chopped spring onion and bacon, and serve the salad on some crisp lettuce leaves.

courgettes à la grecque

If you decide to grow courgettes they'll come at you at such a rate that you'll be wondering what on earth to do with them next. So here's an idea.

350g small courgettes
3 tablespoons oil
1 medium-sized onion, peeled and chopped small
1 clove garlic, crushed
1 tablespoon wine vinegar
6 tablespoons water
6 coriander seeds, lightly crushed
6 black peppercorns, lightly crushed
½ teaspoon Herbes de Provence
Juice of 1 small lemon
Salt
1 large tomato, skinned (see page 150) and chopped
1 tablespoon chopped parsley

First heat 2 tablespoons of the oil in a heavy pan and soften the onion and garlic in it gently for about 10 minutes. Then add the wine vinegar, the water, the crushed coriander and peppercorns, Herbes de Provence, the lemon juice and a little salt. Bring to the boil and simmer for 5 minutes. Then prepare the courgettes: don't peel them, just wipe them, trim off the ends and cut into 2.5cm slices. Add them to the sauce together with the chopped tomato, stir, put the lid on and simmer over a gentle heat for about 20 minutes, or until they're tender. Now transfer the lot to a serving dish, allow to cool, then cover and chill. Just before serving sprinkle with the remaining tablespoon of oil and the parsley. Then all it needs is some crusty fresh bread.

tomato and chilli sauce

350g ripe tomatoes, skinned
1 small onion, peeled and finely chopped
1 clove garlic, crushed
1 tablespoon olive oil
1 teaspoon tomato purée
1 teaspoon Herbes de Provence
¼ teaspoon chilli powder
Seasoning

To skin the tomatoes, pour boiling water over them, leave for 1 minute, then put them in cold water and slip the skins off. Now halve them and chop the flesh quite small. Next soften the onion and garlic in a saucepan with the olive oil, then add the tomatoes, tomato purée, Herbes de Provence and chilli powder, and season. Stir well, simmer gently for 15 minutes with the lid on and then for a further 10 or 15 minutes without the lid. When it's ready, taste to check the seasoning, then sieve the mixture or blend it in a liquidiser, or else serve it just as it is.

white cabbage with garlic and coriander

Serves 4

Cooking vegetables in the oven is only economical if the oven is on anyway, so try to cook this dish when you are using the oven for something else.

1 small white cabbage, weighing about 700g
2 tablespoons groundnut oil
1 large clove garlic, crushed
1 heaped teaspoon coriander seeds
Seasoning

Preheat the oven to 180°C/350°F/gas mark 4.

First take away any stale or tough outer leaves from the cabbage; then, using a sharp knife, cut it into quarters and remove the tough stalky bits. Now, leaving the quarters intact, wash them and then dry them as thoroughly as possible. Pour the oil over the base of the casserole, add the crushed garlic and put it into the oven to heat through. Meanwhile crush the coriander seeds, preferably in a pestle and mortar but failing that you can use a small basin and the end of a rolling pin. When the oil is hot and beginning to sizzle, add the crushed coriander seeds, then the pieces of cabbage. Baste each piece a little, season, put a lid on the casserole and put it back in the oven for about 40 minutes, or until the cabbage is tender when tested with a skewer.

turnips boulangère

Potatoes boulangère are quite well known, but in fact this method works particularly well with turnips too.

900g small (tender) turnips
1 onion, peeled and finely chopped
150ml semi-skimmed milk
150ml hot stock
25g butter, plus a little extra
2 rashers streaky bacon, rinded and chopped small
Seasoning

Preheat the oven to 180°C/350°F/gas mark 4.

First peel the turnips and slice them as thinly as possible. Then arrange the ingredients in a 2.5-litre casserole or baking dish (generously buttered) as follows: a layer of sliced turnips over the base, followed by a sprinkling of onion and some seasoning. Continue with another layer of turnips, then onion and so on until everything is in and you've finished up with a layer of turnips on top. Now pour in the milk and hot stock, season once again, and dot the surface with the 25g of butter. Finally, sprinkle the chopped bacon over the top and cover it all with a sheet of buttered foil. Bake in the top half of the oven for an hour. After that time remove the foil and bake for a further 30 minutes – or until the turnips feel soft when tested with a skewer.

mashed swede
with bacon

900g swedes
50g butter
4 rashers streaky bacon, rinded and chopped small
2 tablespoons semi-skimmed milk
Seasoning

Peel the swedes, cut them into smallish cubes, place them in a saucepan and pour over enough boiling water to just cover them. Add some salt and simmer for about 20–30 minutes, or until the cubes are tender. Now tip the swedes into a colander to drain thoroughly and return the saucepan to the heat, add a knob of butter and quickly fry the chopped bacon until it's just beginning to crisp. Next return the swedes to the saucepan and mash to a creamy pulp, adding the rest of the butter and the milk. Season well and serve piled on to a warm serving dish.

baked aubergines

Aubergines done like this go extremely well with lamb, or they're good on their own as a lunchtime dish with lots of fresh bread and perhaps a green salad.

4 aubergines (about 800g)
4 tablespoons oil
1 large onion, peeled and finely chopped
6 fairly large tomatoes, skinned (see page 150) and chopped
2 cloves garlic, crushed
2 tablespoons finely chopped parsley
A very generous pinch each of ground allspice, powdered cinnamon and caster sugar
Seasoning

For the topping:

2–3 tablespoons dry white breadcrumbs
1 tablespoon grated Parmesan or other cheese
1 tablespoon butter

First cut the aubergines into smallish pieces, then place them in a colander and sprinkle with 2 heaped teaspoons of salt. Put a plate on top of them with a weight on it and leave them to drain for an hour. Then, when you're ready to cook them, preheat the oven to 190°C/375°F/gas mark 5 and butter a shallow baking dish. Drain and dry the aubergines as thoroughly as possible on kitchen paper, then heat the oil in a frying pan. When it's hot, add the aubergines and fry until they're a pale golden colour. Now add the onion to the pan and continue cooking until it has softened slightly; then add the tomatoes, crushed garlic and parsley, together with the spices, sugar and seasoning. Simmer gently now, stirring a bit, for about 5 minutes. Next transfer the mixture to the baking dish, sprinkle the top with a mixture of cheese and breadcrumbs, and dot the surface with the butter. Then bake on a high shelf in the oven for about 30 minutes, or until bubbling and browned on top.

purée of parsnips

If you make this in January or February, when parsnips are really cheap, then I think 150ml of cream will be justified.

450g parsnips
420ml hot water
150ml single cream
Freshly grated nutmeg
Seasoning

First peel the parsnips, discard any of the woody centre bits and chop them up into small cubes. Now bring the water up to boiling point in a saucepan, add the cubed parsnips, bring it back to simmering point, cover and cook the parsnips for about 10 minutes, or until tender. Then drain them, reserving their cooking liquid. Next, either tip them into a liquidiser and blend them to a purée with the cream or sieve them, beating the cream in with a fork bit by bit. Either way, taste and season, adding freshly grated nutmeg, and 1 or 2 tablespoons of the cooking liquid, if you think it needs it.

marrow with tomatoes and coriander

A 700g marrow (a young one will be smallish, with a shiny skin, and when you press one of the ridges with your thumb it will leave an impression)
225g ripe tomatoes (about 4 medium), skinned (see page 150) and chopped
1 tablespoon oil
1/2 medium onion, peeled and chopped
1 clove garlic, crushed
3/4 teaspoon coriander seeds, crushed
1 dessertspoon chopped basil
Seasoning

In a flameproof casserole melt the oil, add the onion and crushed garlic, and soften for about 5 minutes over a gentle heat; then stir in the chopped tomatoes and cook for a further 5 minutes. If the marrow is fresh it won't need peeling; simply cut it into rough 4cm chunks and add them to the tomatoes and onion, along with the crushed coriander seeds. Then add the basil and season. Stir everything around well, put a lid on and simmer gently for 50 minutes, then remove the lid and continue to simmer for a further 10 minutes to reduce some of the liquid.

NOTE: *This tastes good even cold or reheated the next day.*

new potatoes with bacon and onion

Serves 3

Serve this with fried eggs and you have a very quick and simple supper dish.

700g new potatoes, scrubbed but not peeled
25g butter
1 tablespoon oil
6 rashers bacon, rinded and cut into strips
1 large onion, peeled and chopped small
1 clove garlic, crushed
Seasoning

First of all slice the potatoes into rounds no more than about 5mm thick. Then melt the butter and oil in a large heavy frying pan and fry the bacon strips, chopped onion and crushed garlic over a gentle heat until just softened. Now add the sliced potatoes to the pan, season, give it all a really good stir around, then cover with a well-fitting lid (a heatproof plate will do if you've no lid) and leave to cook very gently for about 20–25 minutes, or until the potato slices are tender. Stir once or twice during the cooking to make sure that the heat is not too high and that the potatoes are not sticking to the base of the pan. When they're ready, spoon them into a heatproof serving dish and serve with fried eggs on top.

souffléed jacket potatoes

4 large baking potatoes
Oil
50g butter
6–8 spring onions, finely chopped
150ml soured cream or natural yoghurt
3 large eggs, separated
1 tablespoon chopped parsley
Seasoning

Preheat the oven to 190°C/375°F/gas mark 5.

Bake the potatoes in their jackets, rubbed with oil and sprinkled with salt, for 1¾–2 hours. As soon as they're cooked, remove them from the oven, leaving the oven on and (with your hands in oven gloves, or using a teacloth for protection), cut them in half and scoop out the centres into a bowl. Then arrange the potato shells in a shallow roasting tin (using one potato to prop up another if they don't sit comfortably straight). Now melt the butter in a saucepan and fry the spring onions for 2–3 minutes; then add all the spring onions and melted butter to the potato, together with the soured cream and egg yolks, and whisk (preferably with an electric hand-whisk) until smooth. Taste and season well, then and add the parsley. Now, with a clean whisk, beat the egg whites until stiff and carefully fold them into the potato mixture. Pile the mixture back into the potato shells and return them to the top half of the oven for 15–20 minutes, or until puffed and golden brown on top. Serve immediately – with some home-made chutney to dip the skins in.

irish potatoes

This is an excellent way to jazz up potatoes, especially for serving with cold leftover meat.

900g potatoes
225g green cabbage, shredded
50g butter, meat dripping or bacon fat
1 bunch spring onions, chopped
1 heaped tablespoon half-fat crème fraîche
Seasoning

Put a kettle on to boil while you peel the potatoes and cut them into even-sized pieces. Then place them in a saucepan, add salt, pour over enough boiling water to just cover them and simmer until tender. Meanwhile place the washed cabbage in a saucepan, add salt and pour boiling water on that too. When it comes back to the boil, cook the cabbage for 5 minutes, then drain thoroughly in a colander, pressing out all the excess liquid very carefully. Now return the saucepan to the heat, melt the fat in it and add the spring onions and drained cabbage. Stir them around, keeping the heat very low. Then put a lid on and let them sweat gently without browning for 10 minutes. While that's happening, drain the potatoes, add some freshly milled black pepper and whip them to a purée with the crème fraîche (an electric hand-whisk will do this in seconds). Now add the spring onions and cabbage and their juices, combine them with the potato and serve very hot.

old-fashioned bubble and squeak

Serves 2

It's funny how some humble dishes like this one can be very special simply because of their rarity – so here's to a comeback for good old Bubble and Squeak!

450g potatoes, peeled
1 small cabbage
25g butter
1 heaped tablespoon well-seasoned plain flour
Good beef dripping for frying
Seasoning

Put the potatoes on to cook in salted boiling water, then half fill a medium-sized saucepan with some more salted water and bring it to the boil. Cut the cabbage into quarters, remove the hard stalk and shred the rest. Wash it thoroughly, then plunge it into the fast-boiling water, put a lid on and let it boil for about 6 minutes. Now pour into a colander, put a plate (one that fits inside the colander) on top of the cabbage, place a weight on top and leave it to drain very thoroughly. When the potatoes are cooked, add some freshly milled black pepper and the butter. Mash them (with an electric hand-mixer if you have one) until smooth – don't add any milk, though, because you don't want them to be too soft. Mix the well-drained cabbage into the potato and, when it is cool, take tablespoons of the mixture and shape into round cakes, which should then be dusted in the seasoned flour. Fry them in hot dripping to a good, crisp, golden brown on both sides. Drain on crumpled kitchen paper and serve immediately.

NOTE: *You can, of course, make this with leftover potatoes and cabbage or sprouts; also a little chopped fried onion is a nice addition.*

go with the
grain

It is a fact of life — established by the charts and graphs of the British

Nutrition Foundation – that as our affluence increases, so our cereal consumption decreases. And the same is true in reverse, of course. But whatever our economic condition, grains in all their forms are obviously very important (one need hardly mention that they are the staple food of two-thirds of the world).

I've always had great admiration for the way the Italians, for instance, manage to stretch out their meagre meat rations with the most delicate dishes of pasta. In fact, our household is hooked on it, and we have it regularly once a week. I have investigated making pasta at home, but it is quite a strenuous and lengthy exercise and, at the time of writing, doesn't seem to me all that much of a saving (so I haven't included it here). But bear in mind, when you're buying pasta, that 450g serves 4 people – so it really is economical.

Some people still feel nervous about cooking rice. However, if you follow the instructions I've given here, you won't ever have any trouble. Don't, whatever you do, buy the so-called 'easy-cook' rice. It's much more expensive and, as all rice is easy to cook once it has been explained, you'll have wasted your money!

❋ *Nothing to add to what I wrote then, except to note that there could be shortages ahead which will inevitably increase prices and put rice and pasta beyond the frugal. But let's hope not.*

onion rice

Cooking rice needn't be a problem if a few simple rules are followed. The first rule is always buy good-quality long-grain rice; the second is it's better to measure rice and liquid by volume rather than by weight; and, most important of all, don't keep opening the cooking pot and giving the rice hefty stirs, because this will break the grains, release the starch and cause the rice to become soggy. Don't stir it at all during the cooking, just wait until all the liquid has been absorbed, then tip the rice into a serving dish and fluff it *gently* with a fork.

275ml long-grain rice
25g butter
1 tablespoon groundnut oil
1/2 medium onion, peeled and finely chopped
570ml hot chicken stock or water
1/2 level teaspoon salt
Freshly milled black pepper

Begin by melting the butter and oil in a thick-based saucepan and gently cooking the onion in it for about 5 minutes. Then add the rice and stir it around with a wooden spoon so that it gets a nice coating of butter. Now pour in the hot chicken stock and add seasoning. Stir just once, and when it reaches boiling point put a lid on and simmer gently for 20–25 minutes, or until all the liquid is absorbed and the rice is tender. Empty the rice into a serving dish and fluff the grains with a fork to separate them.

Onion Rice with Herbs This can be cooked as above, adding 1/2 teaspoon of Herbes de Provence or 1 teaspoon of chopped fresh herbs.

Spiced Pilau Rice Again, cook as above, adding with the rice 2 whole cloves, a 4cm piece of cinnamon stick and 1 teaspoon of powdered turmeric.

With all the above methods, if you use brown rice you'll need 40 minutes' cooking time and to use slightly less liquid, as in the following recipe.

brown rice salad

Serves 4

275ml long-grain brown rice
400ml boiling water
3 or 4 tablespoons vinaigrette dressing (see page 148)
3 spring onions, very finely chopped
5cm cucumber, finely chopped
2 large tomatoes, skinned (see page 150) and finely chopped
1/2 red or green pepper, deseeded and finely chopped
1 red dessert apple, chopped but not peeled
25g currants
25g walnuts, finely chopped
Seasoning

Place the rice and some salt in a saucepan, pour the boiling water over and bring
back to the boil; then stir once, put a lid on and simmer very gently for 40 minutes
or so until all the liquid has been absorbed. Now empty the rice into a salad bowl,
fluff it up with a fork and pour the dressing over while it's still hot. Allow it to cool
and then mix in all the other ingredients, adding a little more dressing it if needs it
and tasting to check the seasoning. Keep in a cool place until needed.

brown rice
with vegetables

Serves 2

Serve this with some good cheese and crusty bread to follow and I promise you won't miss the meat.

275ml long-grain brown rice
2 tablespoons butter
2 tablespoons oil
1 large green pepper, deseeded and chopped
1 medium onion, peeled and roughly chopped
2 sticks celery, chopped
75g mushrooms, sliced
450ml boiling stock (or water)
$1/2$ teaspoon Herbes de Provence
3 tablespoons chopped parsley
6 spring onions, finely chopped (including green parts)
Seasoning

First heat the butter and oil in a large, solid saucepan, then add the prepared pepper, onion and celery and cook them over a fairly low heat until they're softened and slightly golden. Now put the rice in a sieve and rinse well with cold water. Drain it, shaking any excess water out, and add it to the saucepan with the sliced mushrooms, stirring well. Cook for a minute or two before pouring in the stock. Add the Herbes de Provence and season, bring to simmering point, then cover and cook very gently for about 35–40 minutes, or until the rice is just tender. As soon as it seems to be *almost* cooked, remove the lid from the pan and continue to cook until the rice is tender and free from any liquid. Then sprinkle in the parsley and the chopped spring onions. Taste and season again if necessary.

buttered noodles with meatballs

Serves 4

1 lb (450g) ribbon noodles (or spaghetti)

For the meatballs:
A 1cm-thick slice of white bread with the crusts removed
3 or 4 tablespoons semi-skimmed milk
225g minced beef
225g minced pork
1 small onion, peeled and finely chopped
2 tablespoons chopped parsley
¼ teaspoon Herbes de Provence
¼ teaspoon freshly grated nutmeg
1 teaspoon salt
Freshly milled black pepper
1 large egg, beaten
Seasoned plain flour
Oil for frying

For the sauce:
1 small onion, peeled and finely chopped
1 clove garlic, crushed
1 tablespoon oil
1 x 400g tin Italian tomatoes
1 teaspoon Herbes de Provence
Seasoning

To make the sauce, soften the onion and garlic in the oil in a pan, then add the tomatoes, Herbes de Provence and seasoning. Simmer without a lid for 20 minutes. While it cooks, soak the bread in the milk for a while, then squeeze out the milk and shred the bread into a large bowl. Mix the bread, minced meats, chopped onion, Herbes de Provence, nutmeg and seasoning together with the beaten egg; form into about 16 meatballs a bit larger in size than a walnut. Roll them in seasoned flour, heat some oil in a large frying pan and fry them until they are browned and cooked through (8–10 minutes). Boil the noodles in salted water with a few drops of oil added for 12 minutes. Then drain the meatballs well and keep them warm. Drain the noodles, toss them in butter and serve them with the meatballs and the sauce.

spaghetti with tuna and olives

450g spaghetti
1 x 210g tin tuna in oil
1 large onion, peeled and chopped
1 clove garlic, crushed
110g button mushrooms, quartered
450g ripe tomatoes, skinned (see page 150) and chopped
1 tablespoon tomato purée
1 teaspoon Herbes de Provence
50g green stuffed olives, chopped
A little butter
Grated Parmesan cheese
Seasoning

First drain the oil from the tin of tuna into a saucepan, heat it gently and fry the onion and garlic until softened. Then add the mushrooms to the pan and cook for a further 2 or 3 minutes. Now add the tomatoes to the pan, then the tuna, tomato purée and Herbes de Provence, cover and cook for a further 10–15 minutes, or until the mixture has reduced to a nice consistency. Next add the olives, taste and season. Cook the spaghetti for 10–12 minutes in plenty of salted water, drain and toss a little butter in. Then season well and serve the spaghetti topped with the sauce. Have some freshly grated Parmesan cheese to go with it.

spaghetti bolognese

DELIA'S FRUGAL FOOD

Serves 4

For the ragù bolognese:
75g chicken livers, chopped small
175g lean minced beef
1½ tablespoons olive oil
1 small onion, peeled and very finely chopped
2 rashers streaky bacon (unsmoked), finely chopped
1 fat clove garlic, crushed
1 x 225g tin Italian tomatoes
1 teaspoon Herbes de Provence
4 tablespoons red wine
2 heaped tablespoons tomato purée
Seasoning

Then:
450g spaghetti
25g butter
Grated Parmesan cheese

Begin by making the ragù: heat the olive oil in a thick-based saucepan and in it gently soften the onion, chopped bacon and garlic for 5 minutes. Turning the heat up, add the chicken livers together with the beef to brown (keeping everything on the move with a wooden spoon). When the meat has browned, add the contents of the tin of tomatoes, along with the Herbes de Provence, red wine and tomato purée, and some seasoning; cover the saucepan and simmer gently for 20 minutes. After that time take off the lid and continue simmering gently for a further 20–25 minutes, so that the sauce can get nicely concentrated. Towards the end of this cooking time, fill a large saucepan with water, bring to the boil, add some salt and then the spaghetti (if you also add about a teaspoon of olive oil to the water, this will help prevent the pasta sticking together). When the spaghetti has sunk down into the water, stir thoroughly, then cover and simmer very gently for 12 minutes. Strain the cooked spaghetti in a warmed colander, add a knob of butter and a few twists of freshly milled pepper, then transfer on to warmed plates. Pour the sauce over and serve with grated Parmesan cheese sprinkled over.

macaroni carbonara

Serves 2

I find this recipe indispensable for a delicious spur-of-the-moment meal that can be conjured up from ingredients I nearly always have in the house.

225g any supermarket macaroni
A little oil
110g streaky bacon, chopped
2 large eggs
2 tablespoons grated Parmesan cheese, plus extra for serving
Butter
Seasoning

Before you cook the macaroni, have ready a large mixing bowl which should be heated in a medium oven (180°C/350°F/gas mark 4). Then place the macaroni in a saucepan of briskly boiling water to which salt and a few drops of oil have been added. Cook it without a lid, according to the instructions on the packet (about 12 minutes). While that's happening, melt a little oil in a frying pan and cook the bacon – not crisply, just until the fat starts to run. Also break the eggs into a bowl, season them, add the Parmesan cheese and beat with a fork. Now put 2 plates in the oven to warm, then drain the cooked macaroni in a colander, whip the hot bowl out of the oven and tip the macaroni into it. Quickly add the bacon, followed by the beaten eggs – and stir it all around speedily and deftly. Continue stirring and the eggs will soon cook and turn slightly granular from the heat of the bowl. Serve on to warmed plates with a knob of butter on each serving and have some extra grated Parmesan cheese on the table to sprinkle over.

spaghetti with olives and anchovies

225g spaghetti
3 tablespoons oil
225g fresh mushrooms, thinly sliced
2 onions, peeled and thinly sliced
2 cloves garlic, crushed
5 anchovy fillets, snipped in half
3 rashers lean bacon, rinded and roughly chopped
2 tablespoons chopped parsley
6 Spanish stuffed olives, sliced
2 tablespoons grated Parmesan cheese

First of all, heat the oil in a thick-based pan and start to cook the mushrooms, onions, garlic, anchovy fillets and bacon gently. Stir them all around from time to time. Boil the spaghetti in salted water with 1 teaspoon of extra oil in it for 10 minutes. Then add the parsley and olives to the other ingredients in the pan and heat them through. Now drain the spaghetti in a warmed colander, pile it on to a warmed serving dish and top with the savoury mixture, sprinkled finally with the grated Parmesan cheese.

macaroni au gratin

Serves 3

110g any supermarket macaroni
850ml water
50g butter, plus a little extra
40g plain flour
1 level teaspoon mustard powder
420ml semi-skimmed milk
175g Cheddar cheese, grated
Freshly grated nutmeg
1 medium onion, peeled and chopped
4 rashers streaky bacon, rinded and chopped
50g mushrooms, sliced
1 tomato, cut into small pieces
Seasoning

Bring the water to the boil in a large pan with 1 teaspoon salt, add the macaroni and boil without a lid, according to the instructions on the packet. Meanwhile melt the 50g of butter in a saucepan, add the flour and mustard, and make up a white sauce with the milk, cooking for about 6 minutes before adding 75g of the grated cheese to melt gently into it, together with some seasoning and a few gratings of nutmeg. Then in a little butter in a small frying pan, soften the onion, bacon and mushrooms together for about 6 minutes. Now drain the macaroni in a colander, combine it with the sauce and the bacon, onion and mushrooms, then place the whole mixture in a buttered 1.2-litre baking dish. Sprinkle the rest of the cheese on top, plus the pieces of tomato. Finish off by placing the dish under a hot grill until golden brown and bubbling.

NOTE: *If you want to make this in advance, you can reheat it in a high oven, (200°C/400°F/gas mark 6), for about 15–20 minutes.*

who needs
meat?!

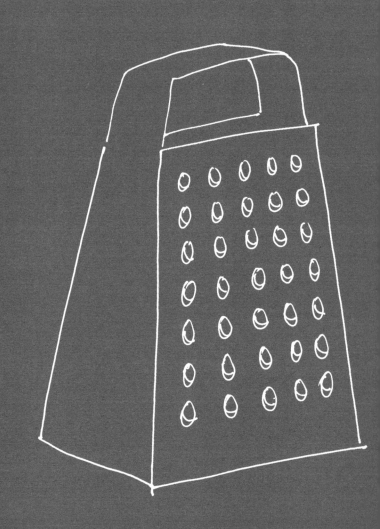

I do, for one. I could never be an out-and-out vegetarian, although

I must admit the thought does cross my mind from time to time. But then all I have to do is conjure up a picture of a steaming steak and kidney pud bursting at the seams with fragrant juices or imagine the sound and smell of bacon and eggs sizzling, and I'm instantly cured.

On the other hand, I also think our national preoccupation with excessive meat-eating is to some extent the result of habit. Once the habit is broken one can live quite happily for days with little or no meat, and I very often do. True, a main meal that doesn't contain any meat (or pulses, which we'll come to later) needs a little more care, needs to be, if you like, a little more special. The scope, however, is enormous: there are literally hundreds of variations on the quiche, just think what a treat a soufflé is, and if you've never tried your hand at a pizza I insist you give it a go now.

As for faint-hearted wives who complain that their husbands only want meat – well, I've never been liberated or concerned with women's rights, but I do think that if you're going to go to the trouble of cooking for someone the least they can do is eat what you cook. So be firm: send him off to buy his own steak and chops and pay for them. If not, blame it all on this book.

pizza dough

225g plain flour
1 level teaspoon salt
¼ teaspoon sugar
1½ teaspoons instant yeast
1 large egg, beaten
75–110ml hand-hot water (i.e. water that you can hold your finger in for a few
moments without burning it)
1 teaspoon oil

Sift the flour and salt together in a mixing bowl and add the sugar, yeast, the
beaten egg and the water. Mix to a dough (you may need to add just a spot of
extra warm water – it depends on the flour – but at the end you should have a
soft, pliable dough that leaves the bowl clean). Then transfer the dough to a
working surface and knead for about 10 minutes until it's silky smooth and
fairly elastic. Now replace the dough in the bowl and rub the surface all over with
the oil. Then seal the top of the bowl with cling film – or cover with a clean cloth
– and put the dough in a warmish place to rise for about an hour, or until it has
doubled in size. Once the dough has 'proved' (that is, doubled in size), knead it
again for about 5 minutes and then it's ready to use. (All this does in fact *sound* a
lot more trouble than it actually is.)

There are many different toppings for pizzas, but here are two combinations that
I particularly like. Of course, you can adapt them, if you want to, and make up
your own variations.

pizza with olives and anchovies

Serves 2–4

For the tomato sauce:

2 tablespoons oil

1 Spanish onion, peeled and chopped

2 cloves garlic, crushed

2 x 400g tins Italian tomatoes

3/4 teaspoon chopped basil

1 large bay leaf

Seasoning

For the topping:

Oil

110g grated mozzarella

1 x 50g tin anchovy fillets, drained and chopped

A dozen black olives, pitted and halved

1 teaspoon Herbes de Provence

1 tablespoon grated Parmesan cheese

Make the pizza dough as described on page 180.

To prepare the sauce, heat the oil and fry the onion until softened and golden; then stir in the remaining sauce ingredients and simmer gently (uncovered) for about an hour, or until the tomatoes have reduced to a jam-like consistency. Then take the pan off the heat, discard the bay leaf and leave the sauce to cool.

Now select a large dry baking sheet (don't oil it) and push the dough out with your hands to a rectangle roughly 25.5 x 28cm – or a round if you prefer. If the dough is very springy, be determined with it. Now pinch up the edges all round to make a sort of border to contain the topping. Then brush the base of the dough with oil, cover with the tomato topping and spread it right up to the pinched edge. Next sprinkle the surface with the mozzarella, anchovies, halved olives, Herbes de Provence and Parmesan cheese, drizzle about a tablespoon of oil over the top and leave the pizza at room temperature for about 10 minutes before baking. Meanwhile preheat the oven to 220°C/425°F/gas mark 7. Bake the pizza for 15–20 minutes. Check that the bread base is cooked through in the centre by lifting the pizza up with a fish slice and taking a look. It's better to slightly over-cook than under-cook a pizza, and always serve it fresh straight from the oven if possible.

pizza with salami
and mushrooms

Serves 2–4

1 x 225g tin Italian tomatoes
1 tablespoon tomato purée
1 teaspoon Herbes de Provence
175g salami or Italian pepperoni sausage
1 small pepper, deseeded and finely chopped
1 tablespoon drained capers, chopped
50g mushrooms, thinly sliced
2 tablespoons grated Parmesan cheese
Oil
Seasoning

Preheat the oven to 220°C/425°F/gas mark 7.

Prepare the pizza dough as described on page 180. Then choose a large baking sheet again and push the dough out to a rectangle as in the previous recipe. Pinch out a narrow border and brush the base with oil. Now either liquidise the contents of the tin of tomatoes or simply rub them through a sieve into a bowl. Then stir in the tomato purée and Herbes de Provence, taste and season. Now pour the mixture on to the pizza base and spread it all over. Next skin and thinly slice the salami, and halve the slices. Then arrange them over the top of the pizza, sprinkle on the chopped pepper, capers, sliced mushrooms and grated Parmesan cheese, and again trickle a little oil over the top. Leave the pizza on one side for about 10 minutes before baking in the oven for 15–20 minutes.

✳ *OK, there is meat in this one – but only a little!*

cheese and vegetable wholemeal flan

Serves 4

For this recipe (ideal for vegetarians) I use an 18cm metal pie plate with a rim about 4cm deep.

For the pastry:
40g wholemeal flour
40g plain flour
40g butter
A pinch of salt

For the filling:
50g butter
1 carrot, scraped and thinly sliced
75g swede, peeled and thinly sliced
75g turnip, peeled and thinly sliced
1 stick celery, sliced
1 small onion, peeled and finely chopped
1 small leek, trimmed, washed and finely chopped
50g Cheddar cheese, grated
2 large eggs
225ml semi-skimmed milk
1 dessertspoon finely chopped parsley
2 pinches of cayenne pepper
Seasoning

Preheat the oven to 180°C/350°F/gas mark 4.

First make the pastry (see page 230) and roll it out to line the plate. Then prick the pastry base and pre-cook it on a baking sheet for 15 minutes. While that's happening, melt the butter in a frying pan and soften all the vegetables in it for 10–15 minutes. Now remove the plate from the oven and, using a draining spoon, transfer the vegetables from the pan to the pastry case, season well and sprinkle the grated cheese on top. Next beat the eggs together with the milk, pour the mixture over the vegetables, then sprinkle with the parsley and a couple of pinches of cayenne pepper. Return it to the oven and bake for about 40 minutes until golden and puffy.

courgette soufflé

Serves 4

This will make a very impressive lunchtime dish for 4 people.

110g courgettes, thinly sliced
110g butter, plus a little extra
3 tablespoons plain flour
275ml semi-skimmed milk
5 large egg yolks
50g Cheddar cheese, grated
25g Parmesan cheese, grated
2 tablespoons finely chopped parsley
2 teaspoons finely chopped chives
6 large egg whites
Freshly grated nutmeg
Seasoning

Preheat the oven to 200°C/400°F/gas mark 6.

For this you'll need a 1.5-litre soufflé dish, buttered quite generously. Start by cooking the courgettes gently in half the butter. Cook them until softened and beginning to colour slightly, then remove them from the heat, season them and leave them to cool. Now melt the remaining butter in a saucepan, stir in the flour and cook for a minute or two before gradually adding the milk, stirring all the time. Bring the mixture up to a simmer, still stirring, and let it cook for about 2 or 3 minutes. Take the sauce off the heat now and cool it by sitting the base of the pan in some cold water. As soon as it's cool enough, gradually beat in the egg yolks, followed by the cheeses, parsley and chives. Add seasoning and freshly grated nutmeg. Now beat up the egg whites to the stiff-peak stage and carefully fold them into the cheese mixture, using a metal spoon. Next spoon half the soufflé mixture into the prepared dish, sprinkle in the courgette slices and pour the remaining soufflé mixture on top of them. Place the soufflé dish in a roasting tin, pour boiling water in the tin to a depth of 2.5cm and transfer the whole lot to the oven. Lower the heat to 170°C/325°F/gas mark 3, bake for 40 minutes, then increase the heat to 200°C/400°F/gas mark 6 for a further 10 minutes.

spinach cream flan

Serves 6

If you can't get fresh spinach, use 450g of frozen, well thawed and drained.

Shortcrust pastry (made with 175g plain flour and 75g fat – see page 230; if using ready-made pastry, the equivalent is 250g)

For the filling:
900g fresh spinach
25g butter
225g cream cheese
150ml semi-skimmed milk
3 large eggs, beaten
2 tablespoons grated Parmesan or any mild cheese
Freshly grated nutmeg
Seasoning
A squeeze of lemon juice

Preheat the oven to 180°C/350°F/gas mark 4 with a baking sheet in it.

Start by lining a 25.5cm flan tin with the pastry. Prick the base, place the flan tin on the preheated baking sheet and bake for 15 minutes. Then take it out of the oven, leave it on one side to cool and increase the oven heat to 190°C/375°F/ gas mark 5. Now prepare the filling by washing the spinach thoroughly and discarding any coarse stalks or damaged leaves. Drain and place the spinach in a large heavy-based saucepan with the butter and some seasoning. (No need to add any water.) Cover the pan and cook for about 7 minutes, shaking the pan occasionally, until the spinach collapses down into the butter. Then drain in a colander very thoroughly, pressing out any excess moisture, and chop it up with a sharp knife. Now place the cream cheese in a bowl and beat in the milk a little at a time, followed by the beaten eggs, Parmesan cheese, some seasoning and a little grated nutmeg. Now stir the spinach into the cream mixture. Add a squeeze of lemon juice and, if necessary, a bit more seasoning. Then pour the mixture into the flan case and place the flan back on the heated baking sheet. Bake in the top half of the oven for about 40 minutes, or until the filling is nice and puffy and golden on the top.

soured cream and onion tart

Serves 4

Shortcrust pastry (made with 175g plain flour and 75g fat – see page 230; if using ready-made pastry, the equivalent is 250g)

For the filling:
50g butter
900g onions, peeled and very thinly sliced
1 clove garlic, crushed
¼ teaspoon dried sage
150ml soured cream
2–3 tablespoons single cream or half-fat crème fraîche
1 large egg
Seasoning

Preheat the oven to 180°C/350°F/gas mark 4.

Start by lining a 25.5cm flan tin with the pastry, prick the base and bake it blind in the oven for 15 minutes. Then remove it from the oven and turn the heat up to 190°C/375°F/gas mark 5 and place a baking sheet in the oven.

Gently heat the butter in a large saucepan, and add the sliced onions, garlic and sage. Cover and cook over a low heat for about 15 minutes, shaking the pan occasionally. Then take the lid off and continue to cook (still shaking from time to time) for a further 15–20 minutes, or until the onions form a soft golden mass. Remove from the heat. Now beat together the creams and egg, and stir this into the onions. Taste and season. Spread the mixture in the pastry case. Then place the flan on the heated baking sheet in the top half of the oven and bake for about 40 minutes, or until the surface of the tart is lightly browned.

leek, carrot and potato pie

Serves 3

This is a complete supper dish made from root vegetables – just the thing if you don't want a heavy meal.

450g potatoes, peeled and left whole
225g carrots, scraped and left whole
50g butter, plus a little extra
450g leeks, halved lengthways and cut into 5mm-thick slices
1 small onion, peeled and chopped
275ml white sauce (made with 40g butter, 20g plain flour, 150ml each of semi-skimmed milk and vegetable stock, a pinch of ground mace)
Seasoning

For the topping:
75g Cheddar cheese, grated
1 tablespoon fresh white breadcrumbs
2 pinches of cayenne pepper

Preheat the oven to 180°C/350°F/gas mark 4.

Bring a saucepan of salted water up to boiling point, then put in the whole potatoes and carrots; bring them to the boil, cover and cook for about 15 minutes. Then drain them, reserving the water. Now return the pan you cooked them in to the heat and melt the 50g of butter in it. Add the washed, drained leeks and the chopped onion, and cook them gently for about 6 minutes, or until softened. Now slice the potatoes and carrots thinly and arrange them in layers in a well-buttered baking dish. Season, then add the leeks and onion. Make up the sauce and pour it over the vegetables. Scatter the cheese, breadcrumbs and a couple of pinches of cayenne pepper on the top, dot the surface with small flecks of butter and bake for about 1 hour.

curried eggs
with cauliflower

Serves 3

If you've got a few spices handy, this dish can be made fairly quickly with just a few eggs and a cauliflower, and it tastes quite delicious.

6 large eggs
1 large cauliflower
25g butter
1 tablespoon oil
1 onion, peeled and finely chopped
1 clove garlic, crushed
2 teaspoons ground coriander
1 teaspoon turmeric
1/4–1/2 teaspoon chilli powder (how much depends on you)
1 tablespoon plain flour
2–3 teaspoons mango chutney
A squeeze of lemon juice
2 tablespoons natural yoghurt
Salt

Begin by dividing the cauliflower into small florets. Have ready some boiling, salted water and cook them in it for about 5 minutes. Then drain them and reserve the water. Next heat the butter and oil in a large cooking pot and gently fry the onion until soft. Stir in the garlic, spices and flour, and cook for a minute or two before gradually stirring in 275ml of the cauliflower water. Now bring up to the boil, cover and simmer very gently for 10 minutes. Then stir in the chutney, lemon juice, yoghurt and cauliflower, and cook for a further 5 minutes, tasting to check the seasoning. At some time while all this is happening, carefully lower the eggs into a pan of gently simmering water, simmer for 7 minutes, then cool them under running water. Peel off the shells, halve the eggs and arrange them on a warmed serving dish. Pour the sauce and cauliflower over the top. Serve with rice and mango chutney.

pancakes with spinach and cheese

Serves 2 or 3

For a complete meal all this needs is a lot of crusty bread and butter and some fresh fruit to follow.

6 thin pancakes (see page 237)
700g fresh spinach
3 tablespoons butter, plus a little extra
4–5 tablespoons double cream
420ml cheese sauce (made with 50g butter, 40g plain flour, 420ml semi-skimmed milk and 75g grated Cheddar cheese)
25g Parmesan cheese, grated
Freshly grated nutmeg
Seasoning

Preheat the oven to 200°C/400°F/gas mark 6.

First prepare the spinach by washing it in several changes of water. Discard any damaged leaves and pick out any thick stalks. Press the leaves firmly into a large saucepan and sprinkle with about a teaspoon of salt. Don't add any water, just cover the pan and cook over a fairly high heat for about 7 minutes. While it cooks, remove the lid once or twice and turn the spinach around a bit with a wooden spoon. Then drain it in a colander, pressing out as much excess liquid as possible. Now chop the spinach, melt 3 tablespoons of butter in a frying pan and add the spinach, followed by the cream. Stir (a wooden fork is good here to break up the spinach) and cook until there is no excess cream and you have a nice moist mixture to fill the pancakes. Taste and add seasoning and a good grating of whole nutmeg. Now arrange an equal quantity of the spinach mixture on each pancake and roll them up; then place them in a well-buttered gratin dish and pour over the prepared sauce. Finally sprinkle the surface with the grated Parmesan cheese and bake near the top of the oven for 25 minutes, until it's nicely browned and bubbling.

baked marrow with sage and cheese

Serves 4

This is an excellent meatless supper dish, especially when marrows are very cheap around the latter half of August.

A 1.4kg marrow
110g Wensleydale cheese, grated
3/4 teaspoon dried sage
1 medium onion, peeled and thinly sliced
3 tablespoons fresh white breadcrumbs
Seasoning

Preheat the oven to 150°C/300°F/gas mark 2.

Trim off both ends of the marrow and peel it, using a potato peeler if you've got one. Halve the marrow lengthways and scoop out and discard all the fibre and seeds. Now cut it into 5mm-thick slices and then halve the slices. Put a third of the marrow in a layer in the base of a 2.25-litre casserole. Sprinkle with a third of the grated cheese, 1/4 teaspoon of sage, half the sliced onion and a little seasoning. Repeat this layering once more, then finish off with a layer of marrow and some seasoning. Next mix the remaining cheese with the breadcrumbs and sprinkle all over the top. Cover loosely with a sheet of foil and bake for 1 hour. Then uncover and bake for a further hour. Serve hot – or it's even nicer served cold if the weather's very hot.

quickening
pulses

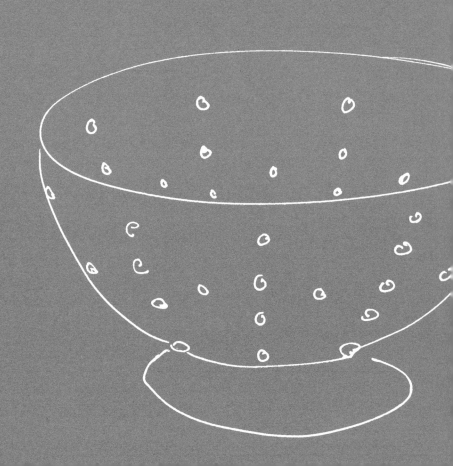

There was a startling report by the Consumers' Association in 1976 which

stated that anyone in this country could survive (food-wise) on £2 per week! What's more, they told us how, and among the top-rated foods for protein and value were the various pulses (or legumes as they're sometimes called): lentils, dried peas, beans, etc.

It wasn't so long ago that these raw materials were overlooked by all except vegetarians. Nowadays, not only are they highly regarded as important sources of protein but also the path-finders of commercialism have begun to use these vegetable proteins to make imitation meat. Never mind if meat is short, they say, we'll just *pretend* we've got it. So Britain was presented with her first samples of Textured Vegetable Protein, and the press with a host of funny 'can-you-tell-the-difference' stories.

Nutritionists (often indirectly on the payrolls of the companies producing TVP) said we were all going to *have* to eat it for future survival. Happily, it hasn't yet caught on (not that producers are deterred – it took 100 years for margarine to be universally accepted). If we can't have meat in the future, then let's not pretend we can – let's evolve in a more realistic direction.

❋ *As I've said elsewhere, we've seen TVP off, thank goodness, and evolved in a more realistic direction. Pulses are now very much a mainstream part of our everyday cooking and eating.*

chilladas

Serves 4

These little lentil rissoles are, in my opinion, even better than those made with meat, and they're delicious served with the Tomato and Chilli Sauce on page 150.

225g green or brown whole lentils
420ml hot water
50g butter
1 medium onion, peeled and finely chopped
1 clove garlic, crushed
1 medium carrot, scraped and finely chopped
1 small green pepper, deseeded and finely chopped
1/2 teaspoon cayenne pepper
1/4 teaspoon powdered mace
1/2 teaspoon Herbes de Provence
2 teaspoons tomato purée
Seasoning

Then:
1 large egg, beaten
Dry fine breadcrumbs
Groundnut oil for shallow-frying

Wash and pick over the lentils, then place them in a saucepan with the hot water and some salt. Bring to the boil, then cover and simmer very gently for about an hour, or until all the liquid has been absorbed and the lentils are mushy. Towards the end of their cooking time, heat the butter in a frying pan and soften the onion, garlic and carrot in it for 5 minutes; then add the chopped pepper and cook for a further 5 or 10 minutes. Next tip the cooked lentils into a bowl and mash them to a pulp with a fork (not too uniformly smooth). Now mix in the softened vegetables, add some seasoning, the cayenne pepper, mace, Herbes de Provence and tomato purée, then divide the mixture and shape into 12 small rounds. All this can be done in advance. To cook them, dip them first in beaten egg, then in breadcrumbs. Shallow-fry them in about 5mm of groundnut oil till golden on both sides, then drain on kitchen paper and serve with the sauce.

chickpea salad

Serves 4–6

225g chickpeas, soaked overnight
225g haricots verts (green string beans)
150ml garlic-flavoured mayonnaise
1 x 50g tin anchovy fillets, drained and finely chopped
6 spring onions, finely chopped
2 tablespoons drained capers, chopped
2 tablespoons finely chopped parsley
A dozen halved and pitted black olives
Lemon juice to taste
A few crisp lettuce leaves
Seasoning

Bring the chickpeas to the boil and simmer for about 30–45 minutes until tender.
Don't salt the water or they will not soften. The topped and tailed haricots will
need 3 or 4 minutes in boiling salted water, then drain them with cold water and
cut each bean in half. Combine the mayonnaise, anchovy fillets, spring onions,
capers and chopped parsley, and add seasoning. Then fold the drained chickpeas
and green beans into the mayonnaise mixture, together with the black olives.
Taste and add a little lemon juice and more seasoning if necessary. Serve on a
bed of crisp lettuce leaves.

boston baked beans

This is how baked beans should be, the real American sort, not a bit like the ones that come in tins.

450g dried white haricot beans
1.7 litres water
1 teaspoon mustard powder
2 tablespoons black treacle
2 tablespoons dark brown sugar
2 tablespoons tomato purée
2 cloves garlic, crushed
1 onion, peeled and sliced
1 bay leaf
350g streaky belly of pork, in one piece
Seasoning

Measure the water into a large saucepan, add the beans, bring to the boil and boil gently for about 2–3 minutes; then remove the pan from the heat and leave on one side for about 1 hour, or until the water has cooled. Now return the beans to the heat and simmer uncovered until the skins burst when you lift them out of the water (which will take around 45 minutes). Drain the beans next, reserving the liquor, then measure the liquor and make it up to 570ml with water if necessary. Transfer the beans to a casserole and preheat the oven to 120°C/250°F/gas mark ½.

At this stage, blend the mustard powder with a little of the measured bean liquor, followed by the black treacle, sugar, tomato purée and crushed garlic, and pour this mixture over the beans, along with the measured 570ml of liquid, some seasoning, the sliced onion and a bay leaf. Now cut slashes across the pork (about 1cm apart) and bury the meat in the beans until only the rind is showing. Then cover the casserole closely and bake very slowly for about 6 hours. During the last hour of cooking, take the lid off the casserole to allow the rind on the pork to crisp a little. Also keep stirring the beans during this last hour and, if things show signs of getting too dry, add just a spot more water. Serve very hot.

dhal curry

Serves 2

Dhal is simply the Indian word for lentils. The best kind to use for this are the red split lentils, which most supermarkets stock.

225g red lentils

1 teaspoon each ground ginger, ground cumin, turmeric and salt

2 potatoes, peeled and diced

2 tablespoons butter

1 large onion, sliced

1 small green pepper, deseeded and chopped

1 level teaspoon Madras curry powder (if you like your curries hotter, you can add more)

1 clove garlic, crushed

1 extra teaspoon ground ginger

4 tomatoes, skinned (see page 150) and chopped

Seasoning

To a saucepan containing 850ml of water add the ginger, cumin, turmeric and salt, then bring it all to the boil. Stir in the lentils, let the water come back to a gentle simmer and cook for 5 minutes. After that add the diced potato and continue cooking until the lentils have turned mushy (making sure the mixture doesn't stick to the bottom of the pan by giving it a stir now and again). While that's cooking, heat up the butter in another pan and fry the onion and pepper in it (over a fairly high heat) until the onion has browned – then lower the heat and stir in the Madras curry powder, the garlic, the extra ground ginger and the chopped tomatoes. Cook for a minute before adding the lentil mixture, then taste, season if necessary and cook gently for a further 5–10 minutes (stirring from time to time). Serve this with rice and yoghurt.

spiced chickpea cutlets

225g chickpeas, soaked overnight in plenty of cold water
2 tablespoons oil
1 onion, peeled and finely chopped
1 small green pepper, deseeded and finely chopped
1 clove garlic, crushed
2 teaspoons tomato purée
2 tablespoons natural yoghurt
$1/2$ teaspoon Madras curry powder
$1/2$ teaspoon cayenne pepper
Seasoning

Then:
Dry white breadcrumbs
Oil for shallow-frying

Tip the soaked chickpeas and their water into a saucepan. Bring them up to the boil, cover and simmer for about 30 minutes, or until they're absolutely tender. Drain well and mash them to a pulp. Now put the 2 tablespoons of oil in a saucepan and gently fry the onion, green pepper and garlic until softened; then beat them into the mashed chickpeas together with all the remaining ingredients (except the seasoning and, of course, the breadcrumbs and frying oil). Do a bit of tasting at this stage, seasoning as necessary. As soon as it's cool enough to handle, form the mixture into 6 patties and coat each one with breadcrumbs. Put about 2 tablespoons of oil in a frying pan and fry the patties to a golden-brown colour. Drain on kitchen paper and serve hot, garnished with slices of raw Spanish onion and some natural yoghurt as a sauce.

white bean
and salami salad

Serves 4

450g dried large haricot beans
1 onion, peeled and stuck with 6 cloves
A few parsley stalks
1 bay leaf
1 clove garlic, crushed
½ teaspoon dried thyme (or a sprig of fresh)

For the dressing:
1 teaspoon salt
2 tablespoons wine vinegar
2 tablespoons dry cider
1 teaspoon mustard powder
1 clove garlic, crushed
150ml oil – olive or groundnut
Freshly milled black pepper

Then:
1 medium onion, peeled and thinly sliced
110g salami, chopped small
1 tablespoon chopped parsley

First put the dried beans in a sieve and wash them under cold running water. Then place them in a saucepan, add enough cold water to come up about 5cm above the beans and bring to the boil. As soon as the water boils, switch off the heat and leave the beans to soak for about an hour. Then add the onion stuck with cloves, the parsley stalks, bay leaf, garlic and thyme. Bring the beans back to the boil and simmer very gently without a lid for 1–1½ hours, or until the beans are tender. The length of cooking time really depends on the age of the beans. While the beans are cooking you can make the dressing by dissolving the salt in the wine vinegar for about 30 minutes, then adding all the other ingredients. To blend them, shake them in a screw-topped jar, then taste and add more salt and pepper if necessary – this dressing needs to be very well seasoned. When the beans are cooked, drain them, and while they are still warm combine them with the dressing in a large mixing bowl. Mix them gently to avoid the beans breaking, then add the onion, salami and parsley, and leave for at least an hour before serving.

lentil, bean
and anchovy salad

Serves 4

This makes a very inexpensive lunch dish for 4 people along with some crusty bread to mop up the juices.

225g white haricot beans
225g whole brown lentils
Seasoning

For the dressing:
8 tablespoons oil
1 tablespoon wine vinegar
1 tablespoon lemon juice
1 small onion, peeled and finely chopped
1 heaped teaspoon made mustard
1 clove garlic, crushed
4 tablespoons finely chopped parsley

To garnish:
1 x 50g tin anchovy fillets
A few crisp lettuce leaves
2 large hard-boiled eggs, chopped
25g small black olives

In advance you'll need to put the beans in a saucepan with plenty of cold water to cover, then bring to the boil, boil for 2–3 minutes and remove from the heat. Leave them for about an hour to soak, then boil them again until *just* soft (probably another hour). There's no need to soak the lentils: just pick over them, wash them and boil them in plenty of water again until *just* soft (about 25 minutes). Meanwhile make up the dressing by mixing everything together in a bowl and adding the oil from the tin of anchovies as well. (Chop the anchovies and keep them on one side.) As soon as the beans and lentils are cooked, drain them, and while they're still warm pour on the dressing, toss them around in it and leave to cool. Then taste and season the mixture well. To serve, place some of the bean-and-lentil mixture on to crisp lettuce leaves divided between 4 plates and garnish with the chopped hard-boiled eggs, chopped anchovies and olives.

curried egg
and lentil patties

110g whole green or brown lentils
3 large hard-boiled eggs, chopped
1 largish onion, peeled and finely chopped
1 clove garlic, crushed
50g butter
$1/8$–$1/4$ teaspoon chilli powder
$1/4$ teaspoon ground cumin
$1/4$ teaspoon ground coriander
$1/4$ teaspoon ground ginger
$1/4$ teaspoon turmeric
1 tablespoon chopped parsley
Seasoning

Then:

1 egg, beaten
Wholemeal flour
Groundnut oil for frying

Cook the lentils till mushy, as in the previous recipe. Soften the onion and garlic in the butter, then add them to the lentils with the chopped eggs, spices, parsley and seasoning, and mix thoroughly. When cool, shape the mixture into 9 little patties. Dip them first in beaten egg, then in wholemeal flour and shallow-fry them till golden on both sides. Drain on kitchen paper and serve on a bed of Spiced Pilau Rice (see page 166), garnished with slices of raw Spanish onion, and eat with mango chutney and a dollop of natural yoghurt.

lentil and split pea loaf

Serves 4

This is nice served with tomato sauce or some yoghurt and is equally good eaten cold with salad or taken on a picnic in the summer.

175g whole green or brown lentils
110g split peas (yellow or green), picked over and rinsed
570ml vegetable stock or water
½ teaspoon Herbes de Provence
25g butter
1 medium onion, peeled and chopped
½ green pepper, deseeded and chopped
2 carrots, scraped and chopped
2 sticks celery, chopped
1 fat clove garlic, crushed
1 large egg, beaten
2 tablespoons chopped parsley
Seasoning

Preheat the oven to 190°C/375°F/gas mark 5.

First bring the stock or water up to boiling point, then stir in the split peas and simmer (with a lid on) for about 5 minutes. Next add the lentils and Herbes de Provence and simmer, covered, for a further 25–30 minutes, or until all the liquid has been absorbed and the lentils and peas are soft; then remove the pan from the heat. Now, in another pan, heat the butter and fry all the prepared vegetables and garlic until golden – about 10 minutes. Then stir the mixture into the lentils with the beaten egg and parsley. Taste and season. Spoon the mixture into a well-greased 450g loaf tin, cover with foil and bake for 40 minutes. When it's cooked, slip a knife around the inside edge and turn out on to a warmed serving plate.

haricot and lentil chilli

Serves 4

Whether you're a vegetarian or not, meals without meat will eventually become a necessity – but that does not mean they can't be just as good, as this proves.

110g haricot beans
110g whole brown or green lentils
50g pearl barley
50g butter
1 large onion, peeled and chopped
2 cloves garlic, crushed
3 carrots, scraped and thinly sliced
4 sticks celery, sliced across thinly
1 x 400g tin Italian tomatoes
1 tablespoon tomato purée
$^1/_4$–$^1/_2$ teaspoon chilli powder
1 bay leaf
1 green pepper, deseeded and chopped
Seasoning

Put the haricot beans in a small saucepan with plenty of cold water to cover, then bring them to the boil and boil gently for 2 or 3 minutes. Remove them from the heat, cover and leave on one side to soak for about an hour. After that, bring them to the boil again, cover and simmer for 20 minutes; then strain the beans, reserving all their liquor. Meanwhile carefully pick over the lentils, put them in a sieve with the pearl barley and rinse thoroughly under the cold tap. Transfer them to a bowl, pour some boiling water over them to cover and leave them to soak for 30 minutes; then drain them, this time discarding the water. Now heat the butter in a casserole until frothy and gently soften the onion, garlic, carrots and celery (but don't brown them). Then add the tomatoes and purée, and stir in the drained lentils and barley, and the drained beans and their reserved cooking liquor (made up to 275ml with fresh water). Now sprinkle in the chilli powder, add the bay leaf, bring to simmering point, cover and continue to simmer for 30 minutes. Then add the chopped pepper and continue to simmer for a further 30 minutes, or until everything is just tender. Taste and season. Add a little more water if you feel it's needed. Reheat and serve with some nutty brown rice cooked with onion.

lentil and vegetable curry

Serves 6

225g runner beans, stringed and sliced

225g potatoes, peeled and diced into 1cm pieces

2 medium carrots, scraped and sliced

225g cauliflower, separated into small florets

4 tablespoons oil

1 large onion, peeled and chopped

2 teaspoons turmeric

½ teaspoon ground coriander

2 teaspoons cumin seeds

2 teaspoons finely chopped fresh ginger (or 1 teaspoon ground)

1 fat clove garlic, crushed

350g whole brown lentils

275ml natural yoghurt

1 rounded tablespoon tomato purée

½–¾ teaspoon cayenne pepper

Salt

Blanch the beans, potatoes, carrots and cauliflower by placing them in a pan containing 1 litre of boiling salted water. Cover and cook gently for 6 minutes; then drain, reserving the water. Now heat the oil in a pan and fry the onion until softened. Then stir in the turmeric, coriander, cumin seeds, ginger and garlic, followed by the lentils (which have been picked over and rinsed), and stir until everything is thoroughly combined before pouring in the reserved vegetable water. Now bring to the boil, cover and cook gently for 40 minutes, or until the lentils are just tender. Next add the blanched vegetables to the lentil mixture, along with the yoghurt, tomato purée and just ½ teaspoon of cayenne pepper. Stir well, and try to push all the vegetables below the surface of the liquid. Bring to simmering point, cover and cook for a further 20 minutes, or until everything is tender. Taste and add a further ¼ teaspoon of cayenne, if you prefer a hotter flavour, and season with salt. Serve with rice.

back to
baking

As I see it, there are two important reasons for home baking. One is that as often as not 50 per cent of the shop price can be saved; the other is that it's almost always bound to taste better. As ever, time is the enemy, but quite honestly how much time does it really take to make a few biscuits, a cake and perhaps a few scones? Grandma's 'baking-day' principle still holds good – perhaps more so now that fuel prices have risen. Once the oven is on, it's best to make full use of it and pop in a batch of baking (provided you have a few airtight tins to keep your biscuits, cakes, etc. in).

I find home baking particularly satisfying and a great incentive to revive that neglected meal, the British Tea, especially at weekends. As for baking bread, if you've never made bread in your life I guarantee you'll find it a whole lot easier than it sounds (not to say cheaper, and so delicious that everyone will eat far too much of it and not be able to manage anything else!).

✳ *In all honesty I can't think of anyone batch-baking nowadays, but the rest of the above holds good.*

strawberry jam sponge

I had always found the classic Victoria sponge very dull and, frankly, not worth the trouble. Then along came soft margarine, and now it takes 2 minutes to whip up a sponge that's light, moist and keeps perfectly fresh in an airtight tin.

110g self-raising flour
1 level teaspoon baking powder
110g soft margarine at room temperature
110g caster sugar
2 large eggs
2–3 drops vanilla essence

Preheat the oven to 170°C/325°F/gas mark 3.

For this you will need a couple of 18cm sponge tins, lightly buttered and their bases lined with greaseproof paper (these tins should be no less than 4cm deep). The size of the tins in cake making is absolutely vital – and no other sizes will do.

Combine all the ingredients in a mixing bowl and whisk with an electric hand-whisk for about 2 minutes, or until everything is thoroughly mixed. Now divide the mixture between the prepared tins, level off and bake on the centre shelf of the oven for about 30 minutes. When cooked, leave them in the tins for only about 30 seconds before turning them out on to a wire cooling tray. When cool, sandwich together with strawberry jam, dust the top with sifted icing sugar and store in an airtight tin.

sticky tea bread

This is unbelievably simple to make – it's dark and sticky and gets much better with a few days' keeping in an airtight tin.

150ml water
150g caster sugar
110g sultanas
110g butter
1 teaspoon bicarbonate of soda
1 large egg, beaten
1 teaspoon baking powder
175g plain flour

Preheat the oven to 180°C/350°F/gas mark 4.

First grease a 450g loaf tin and line it with greaseproof paper, also greased. Then take a large thick-based saucepan and put into it the water, sugar, sultanas, butter and bicarbonate of soda. Place the pan on a medium heat, stir the ingredients together and bring them up to the boil. Then boil for 10 minutes exactly – but don't go away, watch it like a hawk, because if the temperature isn't controlled it might boil over. When the 10 minutes are up, remove the pan from the heat and allow the mixture to cool. Then add the beaten egg, and the baking powder and flour sifted together. Give it a good mix, then place the mixture in the prepared tin and bake it for about 1½ hours on the middle shelf.

irish soda bread

This is a good, easy standby recipe for days when you suddenly need extra bread and you have no yeast available. It isn't a 'keeping' loaf, though, and is best eaten fresh.

225g wholemeal flour
225g plain flour
1 level teaspoon salt
1 teaspoon bicarbonate of soda
1 teaspoon sugar
2 teaspoons cream of tartar
50g butter
275ml semi-skimmed milk

Preheat the oven to 190°C/375°F/gas mark 5.

First take a large bowl and sift the flours, salt, bicarbonate of soda, sugar and cream of tartar into it; then rub in the butter, using your fingertips, until it is thoroughly blended. Now mix in the milk, first with a wooden spoon and then with your hands, until you have a nice soft dough. Knead it for a minute or two in the bowl, sprinkling in a little more flour if it feels sticky. Transfer the dough on to a lightly floured board and shape it neatly into a round. Now, using the back of a knife, score the top of the dough quite deeply, making a cross, and leave it for 10 minutes. After that, place the loaf on a greased baking sheet and bake it for about 30–40 minutes, or until it sounds hollow when tapped underneath. Then wrap it in a clean teacloth to keep the steam in, allow it to cool and serve it as fresh as possible.

sugarless orange and sultana cake

This recipe was snipped out of the *Evening Standard* in 1940 by a reader and it was very popular during the 1974 sugar crisis.

75g margarine or butter
150ml sweetened condensed milk
2 large eggs, whisked until frothy
175g self-raising flour
110g sultanas
Grated zest of 1 orange
1 tablespoon orange juice
Melted lard or butter

Preheat the oven to 170°C/325°F/gas mark 3.

Line the base of a deep, round 18cm cake tin with a circle of greaseproof paper and brush the tin and paper with melted fat. Now place the butter or margarine in a bowl and beat until softened and light. Then gradually beat in the condensed milk, followed by the beaten eggs, a little at a time. Now carefully fold in the sifted flour, sultanas, orange zest and juice. Mix thoroughly and spoon the mixture into the prepared tin. Bake in the centre of the oven for 1 hour, or until the cake shows signs of shrinking away from the side of the tin and is nicely risen and browned. Then turn the cake out on to a wire rack and leave to cool.

wheatmeal shortbread

If you're hard up and need to give someone a present, this would be ideal packed in a pretty tin. It is, in fact, a variation on the usual Scotch shortbread, only using brown flour and sugar, and some ground rice to give an extra crisp bite to it.

150g butter (room temperature)
175g wholemeal flour
175g plain white flour
50g ground rice
50g caster sugar, plus a little extra
¼ teaspoon salt

Preheat the oven to 170°C/325°F/gas mark 3.

Begin by beating the butter in a bowl and gradually working in the flours, ground rice, sugar and salt (using your hands at the end to form the mixture into a stiff dough) – but don't work it too much or the butter will get oily. Then divide the dough in half and roll out each piece to a 15cm round. Now transfer the rounds to a greased baking sheet, pinching all along the edge to decorate. Then, using the back of a knife, mark the rounds into 8 wedges and prick all over with a fork. Sprinkle both rounds with a little caster sugar. Now bake just below the centre of the oven for 40–45 minutes, or until both shortbreads are tinged brown and feel firm in the centre. Then remove them from the oven, sprinkle again with a little more caster sugar and leave till cooled a little before cutting each round into the marked wedges. Cool them on a wire rack and store in an airtight tin.

quick wholemeal
bread

I have adapted this recipe from one given by Doris Grant in her excellent book on wholefoods, *Your Daily Food*. For it you will need a 900g loaf tin (well greased and warmed slightly) or a couple of 450g loaf tins.

450g stoneground wholemeal flour
1 teaspoon salt
1 teaspoon dark brown sugar
2 level teaspoons instant yeast
350ml hand-hot water (i.e. water that you can hold your finger in for a few moments without burning it)

Preheat the oven to 200°C/400°F/gas mark 6.

Carefully measure the flour into a mixing bowl (slightly warm the flour in cold weather) and add the salt, sugar and yeast. Now pour the water into the flour, mixing with a wooden spoon as you do so, then add the rest of the water gradually to make a dough that is slightly moister than usual but will eventually leave the bowl clean. Place the dough in the slightly warmed loaf tin(s), even it out, cover with a clean cloth, then leave in a warm place for about 25 minutes – or until the dough has risen to within 2.5cm of the top of the tin. Finally, dust the top with a little wholemeal flour and bake on a high shelf in the oven for 40–45 minutes if using a 900g tin, 30–35 minutes if using 450g tins. To test if it is cooked, take the bread out of the tin and tap the underneath – you should get a hollow sound. Then leave it to cool on a wire tray.

NOTE: *If the dough takes longer to rise than expected, don't worry, just leave it until it is within 2.5cm of the top of the tin.*

date, prune and walnut loaf

This is a nice nutty wholemeal cake, delicious cut in thick slices and spread with butter.

75g dried prunes, soaked overnight (or ready-to-eat pitted prunes)

100g butter, plus a little extra (at room temperature)

175g soft brown sugar

2 large eggs, lightly beaten

110g wholemeal flour

110g plain flour

A pinch of salt

1 level teaspoon baking powder

75g pitted dates

110g walnuts, roughly chopped

3 or 4 tablespoons semi-skimmed milk

Preheat the oven to 180°C/350°F/gas mark 4.

First butter a 13 x 23cm loaf tin well. Then, if you have soaked the prunes, drain them thoroughly and take out the stones. Chop the prunes into largish pieces. In a large mixing bowl, cream the butter and the sugar together till light and fluffy, before adding the beaten eggs a little at a time, beating well after each addition. Next sift the flours, salt and baking powder and, using a metal spoon, fold them carefully into the creamed mixture, together with any bits of wheat left in the sieve. Now add the prunes, dates and walnuts, followed by the milk, and mix them in before transferring the mixture to the tin. Spread it out evenly and bake for 1 hour, or until the loaf feels springy in the centre and a skewer inserted in the middle comes out clean. Let the cake cool for a minute or two in the tin, then turn it out on to a wire tray to cool and store in an airtight tin.

old-fashioned
seed cake

I think this is best kept in an airtight tin to mature for a couple of days.

110g butter, plus a little extra
110g caster sugar
2 large eggs, beaten
25g ground almonds
2 teaspoons caraway seeds
150g self-raising flour
2–3 tablespoons semi-skimmed milk
12 sugar cubes, lightly crushed with a rolling pin

Preheat the oven to 180°C/350°F/gas mark 4.

Start by buttering an 18cm round cake tin and lining the base with a circle of greaseproof paper cut to fit; then butter the paper too. Cream the butter and caster sugar together until the mixture is pale and fluffy. Beat in the eggs a little at a time, then lightly fold in the ground almonds, caraway seeds and flour, followed by enough milk to give the mixture a good dropping consistency. Now spoon the mixture into the prepared tin, level off the surface with the back of a tablespoon and sprinkle with the crushed sugar cubes. Bake the cake in the middle of the oven for about 1 hour, or until it feels springy in the centre and shows signs of shrinking away from the side of the tin. Cool on a wire rack.

oat crunch biscuits

To make 12

Making these delicious little biscuits at home will cost you half what you would pay in the shops.

125g porridge oats
110g butter or margarine
75g demerara sugar

Preheat the oven to 190°C/375°F/gas mark 5.

Butter a shallow baking tin 28 x 18cm well. Then melt 110g of butter gently in a saucepan, without letting it colour, and mix the sugar and porridge oats evenly in a mixing bowl. Now pour the melted butter into the mixture, and mix until all the ingredients are well and truly blended together. All you have to do now is press this mixture all over the base of the baking tin and then bake in the oven for 15 minutes, or until a nice pale golden colour. Take the tin out of the oven and cut into 12 portions – then leave until quite cold and crisp before removing them to an airtight tin (if you want to store them).

butterfly cakes

Very simple little cakes, these, but it's amazing how quickly they disappear, especially if there are children around.

175g self-raising flour
½ teaspoon baking powder
110g caster sugar
110g soft margarine
2 large eggs, beaten
Camp coffee
1 dessertspoon semi-skimmed milk
150ml double cream
Icing sugar

Preheat the oven to 190°C/375°F/gas mark 5.

Place the flour, baking powder, sugar, soft margarine, eggs, a dessertspoon of Camp coffee and the milk in a large mixing bowl and whisk them together for about 1 minute, or until thoroughly blended. Now arrange 18 paper cake-cases in bun tins. Spoon about 1 heaped teaspoonful of cake mixture into each paper case, putting (as far as possible) an equal quantity of mixture in each case. Then bake in the top half of the oven for about 20 minutes, or until each cake is well risen and has stopped bubbling. Remove the cakes to a wire rack to cool and, meanwhile, whip the cream in a basin with about a dessertspoon of Camp coffee (or more if you prefer). Scoop a little cone off the top of each cake (a grapefruit knife is good for this), place a heaped teaspoon of cream in each cavity, then cut each little cone in half and arrange like butterfly wings on the top of the cream. Finally give them a light dusting of icing sugar and serve.

pauper's
puddings

One thing that I have learned about nutritionists is they rarely agree with each other. However, since they do agree that sugar (white or brown) is not necessary when people are eating normal balanced diets, I assume there is something in it. Dentists, of course, would ban it completely (except that would probably make a few of them redundant).

I agree that sugar-eating is an addiction and, unfortunately, I'm addicted to a certain extent – and very often what is bad for you medically can be good psychologically (it's amazing how quickly I perk up at the prospect of a Mars bar when I'm down in the dumps).

My real complaint about sugar in recipes, though, is that it can so easily kill flavour. Take chocolate recipes, for instance: if a recipe says plain chocolate, then it shouldn't say sugar as well, because plain chocolate already has sugar in it. So my advice is to slash your calorie intake and your budget simultaneously by gradually cutting down on sugar consumption and by looking carefully at all sweet recipes to determine whether the sugar is essential to the recipe or is there to pander to our addiction.

old-fashioned honeycomb mould

Serves 4

This is very light and it separates into 3 layers: a clear jelly top, a creamy centre and a moussey base. Lovely!

570ml semi-skimmed milk
Zest and juice of 2 lemons
3 large eggs
75g granulated sugar
1½ level tablespoons gelatine powder

First place the milk in a saucepan with the grated zest of the lemons. Bring slowly to the boil while separating the eggs into 2 basins. Then mix the sugar into the yolks. Strain the milk through a sieve on to the egg yolks and sugar, and whisk well before returning the mixture to the saucepan. Then stand the pan over a medium heat and stir until the liquid has almost reached boiling point and has thickened to a thinnish custard consistency. Now take the pan from the heat and leave it on one side to cool. Next sprinkle the gelatine into a small cup or basin containing 2 tablespoons of water. Leave it for a few minutes to give the gelatine time to soften, then place the cup in 2.5cm of simmering water in a saucepan. Stir occasionally until the gelatine has dissolved and the liquid is absolutely clear. Then strain it into the cooling custard, mix thoroughly and, when the custard is cold, stir in the lemon juice. Now whisk the egg whites until stiff but not dry, and carefully fold them into the custard mixture. Pour the mixture into a 1.5-litre basin and leave in a cool place to set. To serve, loosen around the edges with a palette knife and turn out on to a plate.

caramelised apples

700g cooking apples
3 tablespoons water
A vanilla pod
10g butter
1 tablespoon apricot jam
Sugar to taste

For the caramel:
75g granulated sugar

Peel and core the apples and slice into a saucepan. Add the water and vanilla pod, cover and cook very gently until the apples are soft. Then turn off the heat under the pan and remove the vanilla pod (which can be rinsed, dried and used again). Now add the butter and apricot jam to the pan and, after a minute or two, beat the mixture to a purée. Taste and add a bit of sugar if you think it needs it. Now spread the apple pulp in a heatproof bowl, cover and chill in the refrigerator.

To make the caramel, simply put the sugar in a saucepan and heat until it starts to dissolve around the edge and darken. Shake the pan gently and continue heating, stirring once or twice with a wooden spoon; continue to cook until the syrup formed is a shade darker than golden syrup. Now pour immediately over the apples and chill again until firm and cold. Tap the caramel surface all over with a spoon to break it up before serving – and some chilled 'real' custard would be lovely with it.

rhubarb and orange flan

Serves 6

The orange in this recipe brings out the flavour of rhubarb beautifully.

For the pastry:

75g fine oatmeal
150g plain flour
2 teaspoons soft brown sugar
50g lard
50g butter

For the filling:

900g rhubarb, trimmed, washed and cut into 2.5cm chunks
75g soft brown sugar
Zest and juice of 1 small orange
1 level tablespoon cornflour

Preheat the oven to 180°C/350°F/gas mark 4.

First of all place the rhubarb in a casserole, sprinkle it with the sugar, the orange zest and orange juice, and bake it uncovered for around 20–30 minutes, or until tender when tested with a skewer; then take it out of the oven and allow to cool. While it's cooling, make the pastry. Place the dry ingredients in a mixing bowl, rub in the fats to the 'fine breadcrumbs' stage, then add enough water to make a smooth dough. Roll it out and line a 20cm or 23cm flan tin with it (reserving the pastry trimmings). Now prick the base and bake the flan case for about 25–30 minutes (temperatures as above); then remove it and increase the heat to 220°C/425°F/gas mark 7. Meanwhile drain the rhubarb in a sieve placed over a bowl to reserve the juice, then mix the juice with the cornflour in a small saucepan until smooth, and simmer for 2 minutes. Now arrange the rhubarb in the cooked flan case, pour the sauce over and decorate the top with the pastry trimmings re-rolled and cut into thinnish strips (5mm wide) to make a sort of latticework pattern over the rhubarb. Now put it back into the oven and let it cook for a further 15 minutes. Serve warm with thick cream.

english gooseberry pie

Traditionally the first gooseberry pie of the season was always served on Whit Sunday – but, whenever it is, it's always something to look forward to each year.

900g gooseberries
175g sugar

For the pastry:
175g plain flour
A pinch of salt
75g lard
25g margarine
A little semi-skimmed milk

Preheat the oven to 220°C/425°F/gas mark 7.

For this you'll need a 850ml oval pie dish – or an oblong enamelled one of the same capacity. Just top and tail the gooseberries, then pile them into the dish and sprinkle the sugar in among them. Now make up the pastry by sifting the flour and salt together and rubbing in the fats to the 'fine breadcrumbs' stage, then adding enough cold water to mix to a dough that leaves the bowl clean. Rest it for 20 minutes. Roll it out, cut a rim to fit the dish and dampen it. Press it in place, then dampen the rim and fit the lid on over it, knocking and fluting the edges. Make a steam hole (about the size of a 10p piece) in the centre, brush the surface of the pastry with milk and sprinkle just a trace more sugar over. Bake the pie in the oven for 10 minutes, then lower the heat to 190°C/375°F/gas mark 5 and bake for a further 30 minutes.

spiced bread and
apple pudding

This is another good way of using up stale bread, especially if you have a few windfall apples around.

About 5 or 6 medium slices wholemeal bread from a small loaf, buttered and
with the crusts left on
25g currants
2 medium cooking apples
1 teaspoon mixed spice
50g demerara sugar
Freshly grated nutmeg
2 large eggs
275ml semi-skimmed milk
A little butter

Preheat the oven to 180°C/350°F/gas mark 4.

First cut the slices of bread and butter in two, and arrange half of these (buttered side down) around the base of an 850ml baking dish. Sprinkle in half the currants, then peel and slice the apples (fairly thinly) and pile them in on top of the bread, sprinkling in the mixed spice and about two-thirds of the sugar. Now top with the rest of the pieces of bread (buttered side uppermost this time) and sprinkle in the rest of the currants, lots of freshly grated nutmeg and the rest of the sugar. Next whisk the eggs and beat them into the milk; pour this over everything. Add a few flecks of butter, then place the dish on the highest shelf of the oven and bake the pudding for about 30–40 minutes. The top will be golden and crusty and the underneath light and puffy. And, in my opinion, it doesn't need any cream.

wholemeal bread pudding

Serves 4

175g stale wholemeal bread, finely chopped into crumbs (in a liquidiser)

225ml semi-skimmed milk

50g currants

25g raisins

40g candied peel, finely chopped

40g shredded suet

40g soft brown sugar

Grated zest of 1/2 lemon

Grated zest of 1/2 orange

1 level teaspoon mixed spice

1/2 level teaspoon ground cinnamon

1/4 whole nutmeg, grated

1 large egg, beaten

A little butter

Preheat the oven to 180°C/350°F/gas mark 4.

Put the breadcrumbs into a mixing bowl, pour the milk over them and mix thoroughly, then leave them to soak for about 30 minutes. Then stir in all the other ingredients, except for the butter, and mix very thoroughly. You should have a nice dropping consistency – if not, add a spot more milk. Finally spread the mixture evenly into a well-buttered 570ml or 850ml baking dish and bake for about an hour.

spotted dick

A very comforting pudding this, especially with some warmed golden syrup poured over before serving.

225g self-raising flour
A pinch of salt
110g butter, plus a little extra
50g caster sugar
175g currants
2 large eggs
A little semi-skimmed milk

First of all sift the flour and salt into a basin, and rub in the butter until the mixture looks nice and crumbly. Now stir in the sugar and the currants. Beat the eggs well, then add them a little at a time, stirring after each addition until the mixture is smooth. Add a little milk if necessary so that the mixture has a consistency where it will drop easily off the spoon. Pile the mixture into a 1.2-litre pudding basin (generously buttered) and cover with a sheet of greaseproof paper and a pleated sheet of foil. Tie securely with string, then steam in a steamer over simmering water for 2½ hours.

blackberry cheesecake

Using curd cheese instead of cream cheese makes this much more economical.

450g curd cheese
4 large eggs
1 teaspoon vanilla essence
150g caster sugar
2 teaspoons lemon juice

For the base and topping:
8 gingernut biscuits
8 digestive biscuits
1 level teaspoon ground cinnamon
75g butter, melted
350g blackberries
3 tablespoons caster sugar
2 teaspoons arrowroot mixed with 1 tablespoon water
1 extra digestive biscuit

Preheat the oven to 170°C/325°F/gas mark 3.

You will need a 21.5cm cake tin with a loose base for this. Put the first lot of ingredients into a mixing bowl and whizz with an electric mixer until absolutely smooth. Then crush the 16 biscuits – a rolling pin and a flat surface will do it in seconds – scoop them into a bowl, and mix with the cinnamon and the butter. Next press the biscuit mixture all over the base of the tin, bringing it up about 1cm at the edges. Pour the cheese mixture in now and bake for about 30–40 minutes, or until firm and set in the centre; then turn the oven off and leave the cheesecake there till cool. The blackberries should be washed and simmered with the caster sugar (but no water) for a very few minutes, then drained in a sieve over a bowl. Add the arrowroot-and-water mixture to the juice, bring to the boil and boil until thickened. Mix the thickened juice with the fruit and top the cake with the mixture when cool. Press some more biscuit crumbs all round the edges. Serve only when thoroughly chilled.

NOTE: *You can, of course, use other toppings. Blackcurrants are particularly nice, or fresh raspberries or strawberries – in season.*

spiced apple shortcake

700g Bramley cooking apples
25g soft brown sugar
1/4 teaspoon ground cloves
1 teaspoon ground cinnamon
1/4 whole nutmeg, grated
75g sultanas
2 tablespoons water

For the topping:
225g wholemeal flour
1 teaspoon baking powder
75g butter
150g soft brown sugar

Preheat the oven to 180°C/350°F/gas mark 4.

First quarter, core and peel the apples, then slice them thinly into a saucepan and mix them with the sugar, spices and sultanas. Sprinkle with the water and cook gently until the apples are soft and fluffy. While that's happening, prepare the topping by mixing the flour and baking powder in a bowl. Now rub in the fat until the mixture becomes crumbly. Then stir in the sugar, making sure that all the lumps are broken down. Next arrange the apple mixture in a 2.25-litre pie (or baking) dish. Sprinkle the crumble mixture lightly over this and bake in the oven for 30 minutes. Serve either warm or cold.

traditional lemon pancakes

110g plain flour

A pinch of salt

2 large eggs

200ml semi-skimmed milk and 75ml water, mixed together

2 tablespoons melted butter

4 large lemons

Lard

Caster sugar

Begin by sifting the flour and salt into a bowl and making a well in the centre. Break the eggs into this well and whisk them, incorporating a little of the flour as you do so. Then, when the mixture starts to get too thick, begin adding the milk-and-water mixture a little at a time – still whisking – until it's all in and you have a smooth batter with the consistency of thin cream.

When you are ready to cook the pancakes, add the melted butter to the batter, and have ready a couple of plates warming in the oven (if you pop the lemons in as well, they'll squeeze more easily). Now melt a little lard in a heavy 18cm or 20cm frying pan, swirling it around to coat the whole pan and the sides and pouring out any excess fat (into a saucer). When the pan is smoking hot, pour in 2 tablespoons of batter and turn the heat down to medium. Tip the pan from side to side to make sure the batter covers the whole base and when the pancake is brown on the underneath, flip it over with a palette knife and brown the other side. Then keep it warm between your two hot plates while you're making the remainder. To serve, squeeze lemon over the pancakes, sprinkle some sugar on and roll them up.

prune and apricot jelly

Serves 4

Because home-made jelly is such a rarity I think this one is special enough to serve at a dinner party.

110g dried prunes
110g dried apricots
50g sugar
1 small piece cinnamon stick
1 strip of orange peel
Juice of 1 orange
1 level tablespoon powdered gelatine

Start this off the night before by putting the dried prunes and apricots to soak in 570ml of cold water. Then, when you're ready to make the jelly, pour the fruit (and the water they were soaked in) into a saucepan, adding the sugar, cinnamon and orange peel, and simmer gently for 20 minutes. Next fit a sieve over a bowl, pour the fruits into it and let them drain thoroughly. Then pour the liquid into a measuring jug, and add the orange juice and enough water to make it up to 570ml. At this stage taste to check there's enough sugar. Now put 3 tablespoons of the liquid into a small bowl, sprinkle in the gelatine and, when it has absorbed all the liquid, fit the bowl over a saucepan of barely simmering water. Stir now and then, and when the gelatine has dissolved and become quite transparent, strain it back into the rest of the mixture, mixing it in thoroughly. Now take the stones out of the prunes; chop all the flesh of the fruits up roughly and arrange it in the base of a 1.2-litre mould. Pour the gelatine mixture over the fruit and leave in a cool place to set.

spiced apricot compote

Unless you're lucky enough to get your apricots picked warm from the tree,
I think gentle cooking gives them much more flavour.

450g fresh apricots (approx. 9), slightly under-ripe is better

2 tablespoons dark soft brown sugar

275ml hot water

1 small piece cinnamon stick

1 vanilla pod

2 teaspoons arrowroot

Preheat the oven to 160°C/325°F/gas mark 3.

First place the apricots, sugar, water and spices in a thick cooking pot
(earthenware is ideal), cover them tightly, place in the oven and let them cook for
about ¾–1 hour depending on their ripeness – they need to be cooked until
tender but not disintegrating. When they're cooked, remove the apricots to a
serving dish using a draining spoon. Then pour the juices into a small saucepan
and extract the spices. Now bring the juices up to simmering point, mix the
arrowroot with a tablespoon of cold water till smooth, add it to the juices, bring
back to simmering point and continue to simmer until the mixture has thickened
to a syrupy consistency. Then pour the sauce over the apricots and serve either
warm or chilled.

index

DELIA'S FRUGAL FOOD

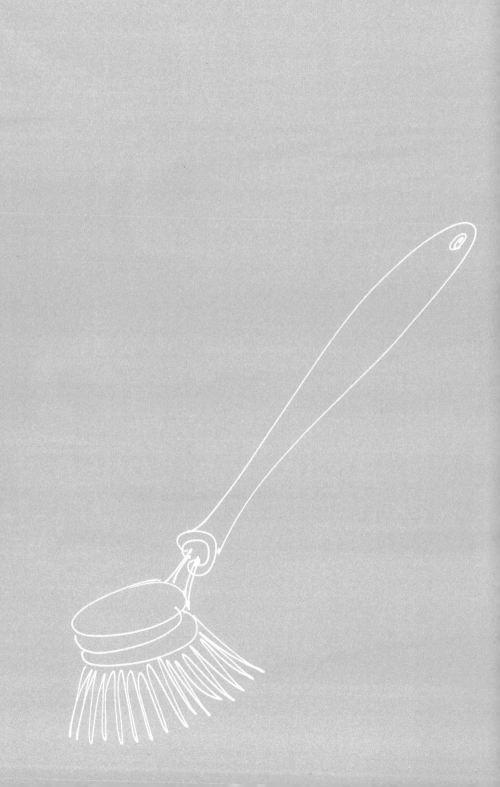